Praise for *The Princi*

"At a time when school leaders throughout the world are facing unprecedented challenges, Fullan has come up with inspirational guidance as to how best to respond. As someone struggling with system change in various contexts, I find his advice both authoritative and challenging. Essential reading for me."

—**Mel Ainscow**, Emeritus Professor,
University of Manchester and Professor
of Education, University of Glasgow

"This book provides essential guidance for principals on how to navigate change and thrive at a time when school leadership has never been more critical."

—**Amanda Datnow**,
Chancellor's Associates Endowed
Chair and Professor, Education Studies,
Associate Dean and Faculty Equity Advisor,
School of Social Sciences,
University of California, San Diego

"Michael Fullan lights the path and continues to ignite our mission as educational leaders. If we have the courage, his words here will show us the way to improve our teams, our schools, our systems, and ourselves to positively impact student outcomes."

—**Dan Wilharber**,
Principal, Scott Highlands Middle School

"Fullan is a master of unearthing the nuances of leadership that help create success. This book and the narratives within highlight successful strategies for system transformation based on the critical role of the principal. What is clear is that if you are to change a system, first you need to change yourself and your own views of what constitutes powerful and enduring leadership. Fullan's analysis and reflections help guide the way to the right doors and toward pathways to achieve the transformation we desire and need."

—**Jordan Tinney**,
Retired Superintendent,
Surrey School District,
British Columbia

"I love this manuscript. It speaks to my personal beliefs as an educator, a coach, consultant, adjunct, a former principal, community member, and, most importantly, as a grandparent of school age children in systems that is challenging for them (almost daily), it speaks to me about people and relationships and the possibility of promise for schools and for the future of leadership. The focus on culture, self-care, humanity and context is central to the work of current school leaders."

—**Ruth Hellams**,
Retired Principal,
Educate Consultant,
Adjunct Faculty

THE PRINCIPAL 2.0

THE PRINCIPAL 2.0

Three Keys to Maximizing Impact

Michael Fullan

JB JOSSEY-BASS™
A Wiley Brand

Published by John Wiley & Sons, Inc., Hoboken, New Jersey.
Published simultaneously in Canada.

For general information on our other products and services or for technical support, please contact our Customer Care Department within the United States at (800) 762-2974, outside the United States at (317) 572-3993 or fax (317) 572-4002.

If you believe you've found a mistake in this book, please bring it to our attention by emailing our reader support team at wileysupport@wiley.com with the subject line "Possible Book Errata Submission."

Wiley also publishes its books in a variety of electronic formats. Some content that appears in print may not be available in electronic formats. For more information about Wiley products, visit our web site at www.wiley.com.

Library of Congress Cataloging-in-Publication Data:

Names: Fullan, Michael, author.
Title: The principal 2.0 : three keys to maximizing impact / Michael Fullan.
Description: Second edition. | Hoboken, New Jersey : Wiley, [2023] | Revised edition of the author's The principal, [2014] | Includes index. | Description based on print version record and CIP data provided by publisher; resource not viewed.
Identifiers: LCCN 2022053691 (print) | LCCN 2022053692 (ebook) | ISBN 9781119890287 (epub) | ISBN 9781119890324 (adobe pdf) | ISBN 9781119890270 (paperback) | ISBN 9781119890270 (paperback) | ISBN 9781119890324 (adobe pdf) | ISBN 9781119890287 (epub)
Subjects: LCSH: School principals. | Educational leadership.
Classification: LCC LB2813.9 (ebook) | LCC LB2813.9 .F85 2023 (print) | DDC 371.2 23/eng/20230—dc03
LC record available at https://urldefense.com/v3/__https://lccn.loc.gov/2022053691__;!!N11eV2iwtfs!u1iNHiiZ9asb7dvJ9URzSYYmD9Vvzlq8mZbogRFbrpvp_w67AWtMFUmi1pcPw3rsVHq5-rcHqDS78zfi$
LC record available at https://urldefense.com/v3/__https://lccn.loc.gov/2022053692__;!!N11eV2iwtfs!u1iNHiiZ9asb7dvJ9URzSYYmD9Vvzlq8mZbogRFbrpvp_w67AWtMFUmi1pcPw3rsVHq5-rcHqFimYG1P$

COVER DESIGN : PAUL MCCARTHY
COVER ART: © GETTY IMAGES|JORDAN LYE

SKY10077394_061324

CONTENTS

PREFACE

PRINCIPAL 2.0 IS BRAND-NEW BOOK, WITH 90% OF IT ORIGINAL. So much has happened in the principalship in the past five years. We are on the frontlines of action, and we have captured its dynamic tension and potential breakthroughs with powerful examples of what the new principalship looks and feels like. I think this will turn out to be a new and crucial era for the heads of schools. They will be expected to build a new internal school and community "system": one that includes students and parents, health and well-being experts; one that develops a local and regional entity addressing poverty, equity, and new learning; one that develops students to be changemakers. Never have the stakes been higher.

I am also aware that the combination of an already broken system, the pandemic in all its forms, climate collapse, and the plummeting of social trust has made it increasingly difficult, and in some cases impossible, for health care workers and educators to survive. It is this scenario that has led many of us to tackle the matter of system transformation using what we call the *humanity paradigm*. This is not an abstract proposition. It is heavily grounded in local development, middle-level mobilization (regional development), and eventually pushing upward to system change. This book—our principals in action—contains many of the elements that will be essential for system change. The immediate period, the rest of this decade (2023–2030) will be crucial to progress, and perhaps even to our very survival. The ideas in this book should be seen as concrete examples of feeding forward into what could only be called the battle of the decade—whether education (well-being and learning) could become a central force for societal survival and flourishing.

Our team of about 10 (sometimes more) works on two overlapping endeavors. One is *systemness*—the idea that systems need greater coherence and cohesion. We recognize that the system is dynamically diverse, which to a certain extent can be a good thing, but currently too chaotic, risking the future of humanity both physically (climate catastrophe) and socially (deadly conflict, and gross inequality). Thus, we work with whole districts, regions, states, and countries to improve education systems that will benefit all. Eventually we want the bottom (local communities) and the middle (districts) to be driving forces for system transformation as much as or more than the state. This is direct work—try to make the change happen as you study and work with the system. It was Kurt Lewin who said, "If you want to understand something, try changing it!"

A second and compatible part of our system work is called New Pedagogies for Deep Learning (https://www.deep.learning.global/). We focus on:

- Certain global competencies (the 6Cs: character, citizenship, collaboration, communication, creativity, critical thinking)

- New learning design and pedagogies that transform the roles of students as learners and all those who work with them
- New conditions at the school, community, district, and state levels

We partner with clusters of schools, whole districts, states, and other entities in almost 20 countries. Above all, we help develop and establish *new purposes for education:* well-being and learning with respect to individual, community, and societal development. Individual academic development occurs within this framework but does not dominate it as it has for the past two decades. Belongingness is a key factor.

In all this work, the principal of course is pivotal—caught in the middle. Are they an agent of the state or the local community? It doesn't help much to say both. But the principalship does give us a powerful entry point to enter, understand, and try to change the system. This book captures the new role of principals required for the demands of an increasingly complex universe and for the opportunities it presents to fulfill humanity and its responsibilities in the rest of this century.

We often acknowledge that some 80% of our best ideas come from the interaction with leading practitioners (including, by the way, young people who in many ways make the best change agents). Again, Kurt Lewin: "There is nothing so theoretical as good practice." I feature such practitioners in eight vignettes spread over the chapters. In Chapter 3, we examine a turnaround example from England; a pivoting success using technology in rural New Brunswick, Canada; and a dynamic transformation of a primary school in the South Island of New Zealand.

In Chapter 4 we check out a quick turnaround of a listless school in California; a major change in culture in a diverse, multicultural high school in Ottawa, Canada, along with how the district context enabled it; and a new, dramatic development of primary school in Melbourne, Australia, that was founded almost 150 years ago.

In Chapter 5 we visit Adlard, the successful school from England, in relation to how it fared during the depths of COVID-19; and focus on a brand-new secondary school in Toronto, Canada, that hit the ground running.

In all these cases it is the principal who enables the local school to come alive—a leader who is equally plugged into the local community and the wider societal policy and social context. Together they produce graduates and citizens who are aware of what the world is facing. They are the beginning, I think, of a potential new era for education marked by well-being and learning where individual, community, and societal development are pursued simultaneously and synergistically.

The last line of the first edition of *The Principal* is: "There is no time to waste!" Well, the all-encompassing COVID-19 pandemic had something to say about that. Where are principals now? In a 2022 survey by the RAND Corporation titled, "Are Principals on the Brink of a Breakdown?" some 85% of principals reported experiencing job-related stress; 48% said they were struggling with burnout; and 28% reported symptoms of distress. Society itself is reeling physically with disastrous climate change and with plummeting social distance between and across many levels (Sullivan, 2022).

The truth is that schools and society have been in a long-term decline for the past 50 or more years (see Fullan & Gallagher, 2020). We live atop a time bomb. The relentless inequality, boredom, and alienation that students experience in school grows as they progress up the grade levels: by Grade 10 or 11, barely two-thirds of students were engaged at school. In this respect, the pandemic has pulled the rug out from under any stability that might have remained. My conclusion in this second edition is that the current radical disruption could turn out to be a good or a bad thing—we know it will not be a no-thing! A lot will depend on the evolving principalship, which I have attempted to capture in this new book.

We are going to enter the system through the portal of the principalship with a view to understanding and increasing the leverage of principals to help change the system for the better. In my mantra of learning most from those doing the job, we are going to get inside the thinking and action of school principals. I am a great fan of *nuance*—seeing beneath complexity, how things tick, and how to enable them to tick better. In the course of the following chapters, you will witness what effective principals do. You will find that principals are expected to help develop and lead a local system of internal cohesion at the school and community level, to be leaders among district and regional entities, and to be able to take into account what is going on in the wider society. Indeed, we will find that the new principalship is anchored in local communities, while recognizing that in many ways they must simultaneously take into account national and worldwide matters.

What would it take to leverage such leaders for further progress? In chapter 1, "The Three Keys: Picking Up the Pieces," we will start where COVID-19 has taken us (and know that the pandemic has not yet departed) and why it represents a major opportunity to redefine our future. The three new keys are described in chapter 1. In chapter 2, "A Long Time Coming," I trace some of the evolution of the role of the principal that take us to the three new keys. Chapters 3, 4, and 5 are based in turn on the keys in action. The final Chapter 6 is about where we go from here. We know one thing: "It won't be static." Read this book like you are a participant in a live action movie.

We are at an inflection point where current forces for societal change will result in a change of direction that the world will take. The trouble is that the direction is precarious and unpredictable. This book is intended to shape the odds toward the betterment of humanity through new learning. Mobilize others and learn together, and don't be afraid to push upward for needed changes!

CHAPTER ONE
The Three Keys: Picking Up the Pieces

CHAPTER ONE

The Three Keys: Picking Up the Pieces

If we can use the metaphor of picking up the pieces, we will find that a lot of the pieces were not worth saving. This chapter starts with a brief account of the three new keys for maximizing positive impact on learning and well-being. I then double back and consider what the pandemic debris signifies for worse and for better. From there, I proceed to whether we have grounds for optimism and provide advice for those principals who want to stay and lead (and indeed those who might want to move into the principalship to play such a breakthrough role). Chapters 2, 3, and 4 will focus on each of the three keys using specific examples from school principals in action with whom we work.

Three New Keys for Maximizing Impact

The original three keys—leading learning, being a district and system player, and becoming a change agent—based on current practice about a decade ago were helpful and were grounded in our knowledge of working with schools and school systems. Things have changed dramatically since 2014. It is a different world now—more ragged, more inventive, more volatile for better or worse. New ideas are crystallizing; some of them are deadly worrying, others exciting. Our team has been close to these ideas, and as usual we are learning from being at the scene of action. We are trying to identify and help those who want to make the best of the situation, indeed learning with those who are working on breakthrough solutions. We present here at the outset the emerging, tentative conclusions about this empirical (and we would say theoretical) work. I portray this work in this section and spend the rest of the book tracking it down and capturing it. The basic framework is portrayed in Figure 1.1.

Lead learners is a democratic concept. It encompasses all leaders from the 6-year-old climate activist to the 100-year-old pot stirrer. Lead learner means two things: being a role model for all others who come within your sphere and helping others to learn especially in interaction with groups focusing on a cause. Put sharply, your job as a leader is to work with others to bring about desirable change *while* enabling the leadership skills of others who can carry on perhaps better than you after you depart. The three new keys will come alive in the chapters

Figure 1.1 Lead Learners

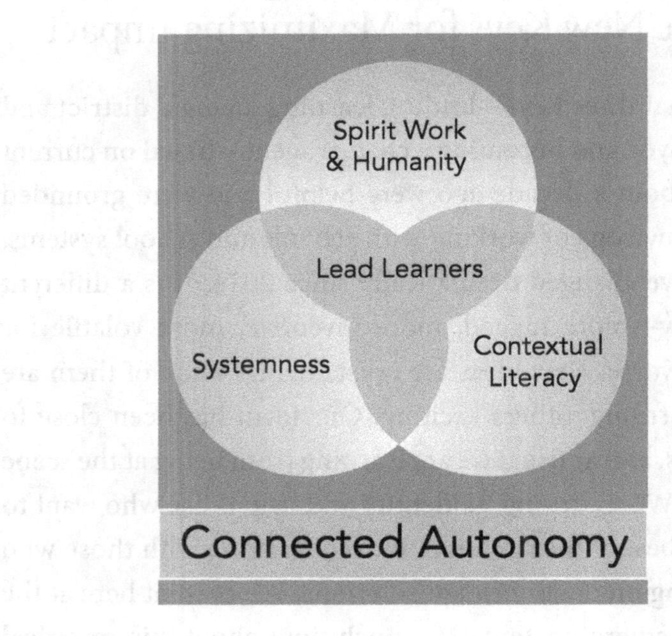

where the examples are presented. They include new exciting breakthroughs around the concept of *spirit work* (Fullan & Edwards, 2022); the powerful *contextual literacy* that nuance uncovered as we followed Leonardo da Vinci's lead to get into the weeds of local culture (Fullan, 2019); and the elusive *systemness* for 30 years, and more following Peter Senge's *Fifth Discipline* (1990). We will also uncover the new dynamic concept, *connected autonomy* (Fullan, Spillane, & Fullan, 2022). As we shall see connected autonomy captures the dynamic equilibrium of being simultaneously autonomous from and connected to others.

But first, we have to address the pieces caused by the world and society going off-kilter in the last 100 years, but particularly the last decade. We will find peril and promise among the innovations, societal developments, remnants, and other spinoffs of the wild period in which we live. What better place to start than the pandemic that has blindsided us in the past four years (has it really been only that long)?

Pandemic Debris

The single best summary I have seen about the pandemic fallout for education comes from my colleague Valerie Hannon and her coauthor of the recent book *FutureSchools* (Hannon & Temperley, 2022). They call their list The Pandemic Shock. They identified 10 "shocks" (one of which pertained to higher education, omitted here). Their list is contained in Table 1.1.

Table 1.1 The Pandemic Shock

1. How enormously important the social function of schools was. On every survey about what (if anything) students missed about school the item that came top was—friends and people.
2. That, notwithstanding decades of expectation that digital technology would transform learning. When it came to it, almost all schools were woefully unprepared. Technology had not been brought into the DNA of schools, and the removal of face-to-face connection revealed how primitive the majority of use was.
3. That although some schools knew and understood their communities, it was revealed how many did not. The home circumstances and real-life conditions of their families came as a revelation to many schools.
4. How the flexibility of *release* from attendance at school had been enjoyed by students, especially those for whom the rigidities of factory-style school routines did not fit.
5. It was revealed how the functioning of economies depended on the safe custody of children to free up parents to work. While homeschooling was revealed as a viable and attractive option for some (a tiny minority), most parents needed others, elsewhere, to look after their children, even as working from home became normalized.
6. It was revealed how the standardized assessment industry consumes time, energy, and money. And for what?
7. Leadership is a key determinant. Whether of countries, cities, or the local primary school, leadership can make the difference: between optimism and hope; vitality or despair; and in the case of the health security of nations, literally between life and death.
8. The equity gap, which was already grotesque, is now unconscionable and unsustainable. Social safety nets were seen to be eroded or nonexistent. Poverty and race were revealed to be preexisting conditions for vulnerability—to viral infection and many other ills. Contrasts could not be ignored in the life circumstances of children—some of whom enjoyed rich, varied, and enjoyable learning experiences during lockdown while others had a full stop to their learning. Some endured increased levels of domestic violence toward both women and children.
9. The occasion of COVID-19 gave many people cause to reflect upon their values—what *really* mattered. Care became priceless; oil became worthless. Nature blossomed and gave solace. Relationships were understood to be at the very essence of a good life.

Source: Hannon and Temperley, *FutureSchool* (2022).

Shock 1: The social value of schools was what students and teachers missed the most. Very few apparently missed learning. (Restoring learning to its proper place linked to well-being is one reason good principals would want to stay or new ones to join.)

Shock 2: In the future, digital technology will play a larger role, but in the absence of good teaching and good leadership it will be disastrous for the future of society. This is a double-edged sword. Now we have the opportunity to use new technology to team up with students and teachers in the driver's seat.

Shock 3: Understanding communities again represents a double message: many communities have desperately poor resources to bring to learning, yet launching a new "Community Schools" strategy as California is doing (our team is part of this) represents a huge new opportunity for school leaders.

Shock 4: Many students enjoyed the escape from the rigidities of factory-style routines. All we need now is the flip side: enjoy the excitement of deep learning. This is another creative outlet for the new principalship.

Shock 5: Safe custody of children is key (and in my mind another aspect of the new community schools arrangement).

Shock 6: The negative yield of the standardized assessment industry is a finding that serves up the power of new assessments focusing on global competencies, which our group and others are now developing.

Shock 7: Leadership is a key determinant that can make the difference between optimism and hope, vitality or despair. New principal where art thou?

Shock 8: The equity gap is grotesque, unconscionable, and unsustainable. Do new principals want to be part of reducing equity, not as a silo proposition as is the current case but as part of an emerging movement to transform society?

Shock 9: Relationships were understood to be at the very essence of a good life. More clarion calls for the good leader.

All this is found in the ashes of the pandemic. Our NPDL team wrote a similar account in a short piece called *Defying Pandemic Gravity,* which contains seven powerful elements: advice to dignify, gratify, simplify, clarify, identify, diversify, and amplify (https://www.deep-learning.global/).

In February 2022, I wrote an op-ed published in *Ed Week* titled "Six Reasons To Be Optimistic About Learning in 2022":

1. Escaping a bad system
2. Recognizing and working with our best allies (students, teachers, parents, principals)
3. Well-being and learning are joining forces
4. New, more powerful forms of learning on the rise
5. Diverse leadership will grow and present new benefits
6. Systems will begin to change

This represents a positive agenda to be sure. Many of the problems were evident before the pandemic, which piled on more grievances. It also unearthed rotten foundations that were previously hidden. And it exposed what many had suspected—that we have the wrong *system*—a matter that Joanna Rizzotto and I took up in another op-ed titled "Whose Abandoning Whom?" Could it be that the system is on the brink of a breakdown, with principals, teachers, and students being collateral damage? We should have seen earlier signs. Time and again when people are asked what they value most at work or in life it is one's peers, good leaders, friends. When they are asked what is most important in life, it is: a sense of belonging, purpose, doing something worthwhile, and making a contribution. The pandemic magnified these shortcomings in the present system and provides an opportunity to take them up as the new agenda as part and parcel of well-being and learning for all (see Fullan & Quinn, forthcoming).

If we pick up the pieces, examine them, identify good pieces from the past, toss away the bad ones, and then contemplate what is needed for the future, we come very close to imagining a better future that would be wanted by the vast majority of society. It is what most students, teachers, parents, and principals would want as well. *Principal 2.0* may be the job description many people find appealing. This positive portrayal is indeed the "three new keys for maximizing impact"! This is the substance of the rest of the book.

A hint about where we are going. The new role for the principal is developer of the internal system. The internal system is the students, parents, teachers, community vis-à-vis the external system—the hierarchy of policies and requirements coming from the system—the state, and regional authorities.

·CHAPTER ONE·

The Three Keys: Picking Up the Pieces

CHAPTER TWO

A Long Time Coming

·CHAPTER THREE·

Spirit Work: The First Key for Maximizing Impact

·CHAPTER FOUR·

Contextual Literacy: The Second Key for Maximizing Impact

·CHAPTER FIVE·

Systemness in Action: The Third Key for Maximizing Impact

·CHAPTER SIX·

Future Making

CHAPTER · TWO

A Long Time Coming

A serious discussion about the deep leadership role of principals has been a long time coming. We have spent at least 30 years bouncing from one extreme to another on the false dichotomy of *principal as instructional leader* versus *principal as autonomous school leader*. We now know—a classic change finding actually—that neither works. The former is too narrow, and the latter too vague. Both solutions are too blatant; that is, they lack nuance—a hint here about where we are going. If you want solid beneficial change, you need leadership that enables focused interaction over time to develop shared solutions that exemplify *specificity without imposition*. Keep that as a tantalizing thought while we briefly revisit the 2014 edition of *The Principal*. After that I will summarize in current terms what is still missing in the principalship.

The early pages of the first edition explored the concept of *too broad, too narrow*. The following section contains excerpts that are slightly edited and adapted from the original. We have had many false starts since the turn of the century, when No Child Left Behind legislation in the United States signaled a period of tightening the line of leadership to improve results in student learning. This chapter shows why this approach failed, which sets the stage for the new, more powerful forms of leadership exemplified in the eight vignettes across subsequent chapters.

Too Broad, Too Narrow

Stubborn problems set us oscillating back and forth, like an unconfident boxer who weaves from side to side, believing they lack the punch to win the bout. Over the years, educators and their mentors have cycled through a "too broad" period of supposing that what has come to be known (vaguely at the time) as "transformative leadership" must be the key, then back to a "too narrow" period in which principals are expected to be right in their giving specific feedback to as many individual teachers as they can. If you have been in education long enough, you can get hit by the same pendulum more than once!

If you've been a principal for a while, you will have experienced times when transformative leadership has been highlighted. Leaders are to become generally attuned to the moral imperative of raising the bar and closing the gap as they inspire teachers and others to new levels of energy and commitment. The shared mission was meant to become a rallying point for teachers *somehow* to accomplish things never before achieved. It was all *very* broad indeed. The trouble was it was vague and unclear about where to start and what to do. Specificity and clarity were missing commodities.

In reality, the evidence shows that the transformative leadership concept and movement simply didn't work because they lacked detail and strategies for getting at the specifics of good change. Viviane Robinson of the University of Auckland is a leading international education researcher specializing in leadership and school improvement. Conducting an in-depth meta-analysis of 22 studies, she and her colleagues found that the impact of transformative leadership was a puny 0.11 in effect size on student achievement (Robinson, Lloyd, & Rowe, 2008). (An effect size is a statistical measure of the degree of relationship between two variables—an effect size below 0.40 is considered to be weak or insignificant.) Basically, the authors found that creating a general inspiring vision attempting to instill motivation in teachers to join the cause was not specific enough to produce actual results. One can readily surmise that creating broad, even inspiring messages do not help much absent the actual mechanics of getting to where you want to go.

Robinson saw more promise at the narrower end. She found that what she called *instructional leadership* had a significant (but still not impressive) effect size of 0.42. This finding and those of others have indeed raised the expectation that principals should become instructional leaders. My own conclusion is that principals can engage in too much instructional leadership or, even more disturbing, to suggest that principals can have too much moral imperative (defined as a deep and relentless commitment to raising the bar and closing the gap in learning for all students without developing the specifics about how to do this). In any case, the shift to instructional leadership has led the principalship down an unproductively narrow path of being expected to micromanage or otherwise directly affect instruction.

The narrow view raises two problems: first, in complex matters, you can't really micromanage to good effect; second, it can be incredibly time-consuming for principals, diverting them from doing other things that can shape learning more powerfully. Supervising individual teachers into better performance is simply impossible if you have a staff of, say, more than 20 teachers. Principals who find themselves in districts that require that they spend, say, two days per week, observing in classrooms will be less effective overall because they can't influence very many teachers in any given time period; they can't be experts in all areas of instruction; and they will end up neglecting other aspects of their role that would make a bigger difference, such as developing the professional capital of teachers as a group, along with other key aspects of leadership essential for motivating people to work together with the leader and others (see Chapter 3).

A similar point had been made in an article by Richard DuFour and Robert Marzano (2009). DuFour advanced through a long, distinguished career as teacher, principal, and superintendent to become an education writer and consultant who has left us a great legacy of insights. Marzano is another leading researcher and consultant whose practical translations of current research and theory into classroom strategies are internationally known and widely practiced. As they put it, "Time devoted to building the capacity of teachers to work in teams is far better spent than time devoted to observing individual teachers" (DuFour & Marzano, 2009, p. 67). But somehow these observations have been overshadowed by the accountability juggernaut. I asked Lyle Kirtman, who has spent the last decade identifying the competencies of effective education leaders (more about his findings toward the end of this chapter), if he had encountered the problem of too narrow a focus on instructional leadership. Within a nanosecond he fired off two examples:

> One principal in a wealthy community received a vote of no confidence from her faculty. Her focus was on instructional leadership and the use of data to improve results for all her students. Her superintendent interviewed ten faculty members and found that her communication skills,

> her empathy for faculty and students, a lack of support for teachers on parent complaints, and her relationship to her principal peers in the district were extremely poor. Her leadership style was more on content and data and not strong in dealing with people. She was very angry about the superintendent's viewpoint because she believed that her instructional skills were exceptional and that it was difficult teachers that were the problem.
>
> Another principal in a suburban district was focused on instruction and data analysis for students. She was confrontational with teachers about how they needed to improve. There were constant complaints from teachers about her lack of overall leadership skills. The superintendent finally received a vote of no confidence from the faculty and removed her as principal. (personal communication, March 2013)

You could say that these two principals were not very good leaders—that they lacked emotional intelligence or even good managerial qualities—and that is the point. A narrow focus on instructional leadership and student achievement can shut out other dimensions of leading learning. And, strange as it may seem, being deeply passionate can lead to blind spots if you become overbearing—a phenomenon that Kaplan and Kaiser (2013) discuss in their book *Fear Your Strengths*.

In short, it is easy to go overboard on instructional leadership. Principals need to be specifically involved in instruction so that they are knowledgeable about its nature and importance, but if they try to run the show down to the last detail it will have a very brief run on Broadway indeed.

Principal Autonomy and Micromanaging

Another false step that is appealing on the surface is to strip away the constraints of bureaucracy by giving the school principal more autonomy in exchange for delivered accountability. Principals can be given more discretion over hiring staff and more flexibility with respect to budget and resources. New York City used this model, as have certain states in Australia. In these cases, individual schools are granted greater autonomy and are expected to deliver strong accountability through teacher appraisal and student test results. This deal with the devil has several problems. First, not many schools have the capacity in the first place, so they could hardly do better if left on their own. Second, those who are most advantaged often are the first to respond, creating an even greater gap between the haves and the have-nots. Third, it's not that good a deal anyway. It puts everyone constantly on guard and makes it impossible for isolated successes to play any part in promoting a larger, more lasting solution. Thus, individual autonomy of schools is no more of a solution than individual autonomy of teachers.

The devil loves to tempt individual principals to go their own way. Autonomy is almost always preferable to being in a bad relationship (for example, a stifling bureaucracy), but the truth is that a good relationship is better still, which is where my argument is heading. In the rest of the book, I will make the case that connected learning, within and across schools and systems, is the only way for whole systems to improve and keep improving. Connected autonomy as I will call it (Fullan, Spillane & Fullan, 2022).

The main point here is that principals are being led down a narrow path of instructional leadership that will ultimately prove futile. They are being called on to micromanage, whereby they go after instruction in detail, teacher by teacher. DuFour and Mattos (2013), both former principals engaged in research, comment on what Race to the Top precision has spawned in Tennessee, one of the first states to win the grant. The model that the state proposed (and was funded to carry out) "calls for 50 percent of a teacher's evaluation to be based on principal observations, 35 percent on student growth, and 15 percent on student achievement data" (p. 36). DuFour and Mattos summarize the new role:

> Principals or evaluators must observe new teachers six times each year and licensed teachers four times each year, considering one or more of four areas—instruction, professionalism, classroom environment, and planning. These four areas are further divided into 116 subcategories. Observations are to be preceded by a pre-conference, in which the principal and the teacher discuss the lesson, and followed by a post-conference, in which the principal shares his or her impressions of the teacher's performance. Principals must then input data on the observation using the state rubric for assessing teachers. Principals report that the process requires four to six hours for each observation. (2013, p. 36)

One can readily surmise that if you are a principal in such a system, under intense scrutiny to cover all your assignments, you will either burn out or learn to go through the procedures superficially. In either case, actual improvement is the casualty. If it is any consolation to the Tennessees of the world, it is easier to shift from such micromanaging to what we call developing the professional capital of one's teachers than it is to shift from excessive individualism (and get anywhere at all). With excessive individualism, or greater autonomy, one does not necessarily develop expertise, whereas micromanagers at least develop expertise in instruction that can be useful in the service of collaborative work.

A good example of the contrast between autonomy and focused collaboration can be found in David Kirp's (2013) revealing study of Union City, New Jersey. Union City is a poor, crowded, Latino community that for much of the last quarter of the last century was the poorest-performing district in the state. That changed in the last decade. By 2011, 89.4% of the Union City students graduated from high school—15% more than the national average. Among other things, the Union City district got the principalship right, finding that "just right" productive ground between micromanaging and excessive autonomy. Kirp comments on nearby Trenton, a city that embraced what he calls the great leader theory (excessive individualism, in my words), whereby superstar principals were hired and given autonomy in exchange for delivering results. The results didn't materialize. In Trenton from 1999 to 2008, the percentage of students passing Grade 8 math tests rose from 18.2% to 21.9%. (By comparison, in Union City, the corresponding figures were 42% to 71%.)

Union City has been successful because it focuses on developing and employing the professional capital of its teachers, principals, and schools (Hargreaves & Fullan, 2012). Kirp (2013) refers to Les, a principal who does understand her job in this fashion:

> Aside from observing and evaluating the teachers, Les needs to help them improve. One strategy is to break through the isolation of the classrooms, encouraging teachers to work together, jointly devise projects for their students, and talk about what's working well in their classrooms and what isn't. Such collaboration, the evidence shows, can make a substantial difference in the quality of instruction. (p. 54)

Very few districts or states seem to grasp the critical distinction between focused collaboration and detailed micromanaging. The road to perdition that I am describing is paved with good intentions. Take the document from New Jersey, "Student Growth Objectives: Developing and Using Practical Measures of Student Learning" (New Jersey Department of Education, 2013). There follows quite a good, rational discussion of specific and measurable objectives linked to standards, based on prior learning, measured between two points in time. Teachers are then required to develop student growth objectives (SGOs) and have them approved by the principal (or the principal's designee) by November, with any changes completed and approved by February; finally, the teacher's supervisor scores the SGO, with the rating being discussed at the annual summary conference.

What starts as a reasonable proposition—let's be clear, know the individual students, and provide instruction accordingly—turns into one big compliance nightmare for teachers and principals alike. A good idea becomes an odious task. There is only one thing worse than having to carry out an odious task: having to supervise those carrying out such tasks. This type of well-intentioned compliance regimen is being replicated around the country in the name of accountability. It is nothing but a time and energy drain for all involved. The cure becomes the disease, and it is ruining the principalship, not to mention student learning itself. In addition, the entire premise is individualistic. There is nothing in the strategy about developing the group. It's as if the system has unlimited supervisory capacity and that principals have all the time in the world to change teachers one at a time.

Large-scale compliance diktats minimize impact—just the opposite of what is intended. To be clear, there are good ideas in the SGO document, but they cannot be fulfilled by compliance-driven specificity. The goodness gets squandered as principals and teachers find themselves going through the contortions of compliance or the distortions of defiance. Far better to set the conditions for maximizing impact that I describe in this book, whereby principals and teachers are helped to develop their professional capital and corresponding expertise and commitments and then scrutinize for quality and accountability, all in a transparent manner. As Kirtman (2013) found about effective leaders, they are low on compliance for the sake of compliance and high on influence for the sake of learning. They influence others to learn and to take related action. Commitment always trumps compliance as a change strategy.

To return to the present, David Kirp and his colleagues have once more proven the point about what specific system-wide reform looks like in their 2022 book (titled *Disrupting Disruption*) of three districts in the United States. *Disrupting Disruption* shines a light on school systems that have overcome the fragmentation, isolation, and lost learning opportunities among teachers and schools. Rather than simply describing best practices in the abstract, the authors look closely at three districts—Union, Oklahoma; Union City, New Jersey; and Roanoke, Virginia—where educators have broken down these barriers. Those efforts have borne fruit—in each instance, graduation rates have consistently improved and the achievement gap closed. These impressive results aren't one-shot events. They have persisted over a sustained period for a racially and socioeconomically diverse student population. The fact that these schools and communities are dealing with challenges related to poverty, linguistic and cultural differences, and racial discrimination makes these accounts especially important. Far too often, these factors have become a convenient rationale for the persistence of mediocrity in many schools and outright failure in others. Plainly, it doesn't have to be that way (Kirp et al., 2022, p. ii). Kirp and his group do find success in heterogenous group but these new conditions are rare.

Alas, the problem is that Kirp's districts and many other individual districts and schools are *the exceptions!* The overall system itself is not improving—if anything, the system is getting worse. Moreover, Kirp's exceptional districts are not engaging in deep learning with respect to global competencies, and the outcomes of integrating well-being and new learning beyond academic skills.

Failure to Improve

I continue to work with Lyle Kirtman, who has a wonderful way of exposing basic problems. Kirtman studies leaders up close: what they *actually do;* equally important, what they *fail to do.*

His research is exceptionally grounded with observation instruments focusing on their behavior, not what they *say* they believe in or do. Figure 2.1 summarizes his most recent findings.

The findings in Figure 2.1 capture what we have found to be the case in our system and deep learning work that form the basis of Chapters 3, 4, and 5. First, as we concluded earlier in this chapter, education leaders need broader skills and competencies beyond instruction. Keeping with the theme of this book and the upcoming chapters, these broader skills will need to be specific not vague.

Second, top-down leaders do not create sustainable change. This is our system work. Tim Brighouse and Mick Waters (2021) in *About Our Schools,* in a truly magnum opus, interviewed or otherwise studied the policies of all the secretaries of state (national ministers of education) in England since 1975. They found what was essentially a steady stream of ad hoc initiatives

Figure 2.1 Research Findings on Leadership Effectiveness That Might Surprise You, Kirtman, 2021, unpublished.

- Leaders need broader (beyond instruction) leadership skills and competencies.
- Top-down leaders do not create sustainable change.
- Most leaders are cautious and don't have a high sense of urgency.
- External networking and partnerships increase results.
- Motivating staff gets better results than current evaluation process.
- Stress and defensiveness from data/critical feedback decreases results.
- Leaders who are overly concerned with others often get lower results.
- Focus on compliance and rule following decreases results.

rained down on local authorities and schools over the 45-year period that they examined. This mega finding alone hints at the critical role of local principals—screening ad hoc initiatives as they go about forging local priorities.

Third, most leaders are cautious and do not have a high sense of urgency. Whatever the vision statements say, the actions do not demonstrate urgency. Perhaps it is because many leaders do not know what to do or know they will face opposition unfounded or otherwise.

Fourth, external networking and partnerships increase results. Kirtman found that principals who focus on instruction internal to the school but did not get out much were less effective in influencing results compared with principals who focused internally but also networked externally (go outside to get better inside, as we say).

Fifth, evaluation is not much of a motivator. It is better to motivate people with purpose, good colleagues, and a chance to make a difference. And, believe it or not, specificity can work, as long as it is not imposed. Under conditions of trust, transparency, and interaction people do respond.

Sixth, strengths and defensiveness from data and critical feedback decrease results. Data do not speak for themselves. There are nuances and contexts to be understood, relationships to be built, and consideration of which pathways may be best to follow.

Seventh, those who are overly concerned with others often get lower results. This finding connects especially with the third point in Figure 2.1—lack of a sense of urgency. Concern about what others might think, especially one's superiors, can hamper one's actions. Take the mid-term view and work toward results.

Effective principals take calculated risks as they go about spirit work of value to their schools and communities.

Finally, focusing on compliance and rule following decreases results. Large-scale compliance diktats minimize impact—just the opposite of what is intended. There are just too many things to attend to, and trying to do so literally either burns out leaders or gets done superficially. Commitment always trumps compliance as a change strategy.

Conclusion

The end result is the findings from the RAND study reported in the Preface. The majority of school leaders are burning or stressing out; many are leaving the profession. Yet it could be different—even under (nay, especially under) current circumstances where certain principals take calculated risks amid the chaos of pandemic disruption. Recall the *Six Reasons To Be Optimistic About Learning in 2022* (see Chapter 1). Reason number 2 was "recognizing and working with our best allies (students, teachers, parents)." The opportunity for change is often greatest when things are broken and when there are cracks in the system. The leadership framework we have developed in the past few years, including within the pandemic, offers numerous opportunities to build a new learning system. Those principals and teachers who have stayed, those who might be attracted to a profession that could become a crucial societal resource, those places that have started down this new pathway could represent a golden opportunity—to reshape learning that focuses on deep learning, and on the individual, and collective development crucial to the human condition. The principals main job is to develop the *internal system* at the school and community levels while sorting out external demands and opportunities. To become an effective system player you have to have the internal house in order.

In sum, new more powerful roles for school leaders have indeed been a long time coming (and it's not here yet). But recently we do have a comprehensive new three-part framework that has been generated by practitioners and researchers working under increasingly difficulty conditions. Sometimes developing good ideas on the edge of bad times is the best way forward. Let's see.

We can now turn to the new three new keys for leadership—*spirit work, contextual literacy,* and *systemness*—along with the eight principal vignettes. Together they form the substance of the next three chapters.

CHAPTER ONE

The Three Keys: Picking Up the Pieces

CHAPTER TWO

A Long Time Coming

CHAPTER THREE

Spirit Work: The First Key for Maximizing Impact

CHAPTER FOUR

Contextual Literacy: The Second Key for Maximizing Impact

CHAPTER FIVE

Systemness in Action: The Third Key for Maximizing Impact

CHAPTER SIX

Future Making

CHAPTER · THREE

Spirit Work: The First Key for Maximizing Impact

As school systems (and society) worsened over the past decade, in a real sense we witnessed the deterioration of society. Physical calamities were happening and compounding almost every day. Societal forces for good were obviously weakening—just as one indicator, the degree of social trust, plummeted in the United States from some 65% saying that they trusted other groups to 30%+ (Putnam & Garrett, 2020). For the first time societal collapse was no longer seen as theoretical or far into the future.

Those in schools felt the immediacy more than most. Besides, school is becoming less and less relevant with almost two-thirds of the students finding it boring or alienating by the time they reached Grade 10 or 11 (Malin, 2018). All this before COVID-19. Chapter 1 discussed the nine indicators of the devastation wreaked by the pandemic as identified by Hannon and Temperley (2022). Go back and take a look at that list. Disruption for sure—but look more closely and you can find the potential for new transformation. Out of the ashes comes a sense of dread but also a potential new spirit that returns many of us to what the role of education should be in a complex challenging world.

I have long focused on, worked with, and written about the moral purpose of schooling: the need to raise the bar and close the gap for all students regardless of background in terms of student achievement. But the world is changing rapidly, and student achievement by itself seemed no longer adequate (nor can it be achieved by doubling down on the pressure of tests and assessment). We began to look closer and saw that the underlying *humanity* of our existence was at stake. In the right drivers analysis, I called this issue the humanity paradigm (Fullan, 2021; see also Fullan & Quinn, forthcoming). We are in effect moving to something as fundamental as the human condition.

This theme of well-being and learning—"good at learning, good at life" formed the basis of our deep learning work that evolved from 2014 (https://www.deep-learning.global/). In late 2018, I had a chance to join with Mark Edwards, a former superintendent from the northeast United States, to study seven school districts across the country that seemed to be doing well with all its students despite the growing difficulties in society, including the rapidly growing presence and spread of COVID-19. We found amazing activities across the districts, publishing the results (Fullan & Edwards, 2022). Leaders at all levels in these districts showed enormous care about their students, parents, and communities. They deeply loved their communities and the people in them. Moreover, they knew they had to work relentlessly and collaboratively to have any chance of success. We titled our book *Spirit Work and the Science of Collaboration*.

The leaders in these seven districts did not use the term *spirit work*, but as soon as we labeled it they all said, pretty much simultaneously, that it is exactly what the work entails. Later, in 2022, the British Columbia Superintendents Association, which included an Indigenous leaders' subgroup, labeled their set of leadership competencies as *spirit work*. We define spirit work in Figure 3.1.

Figure 3.1 Spirit Work

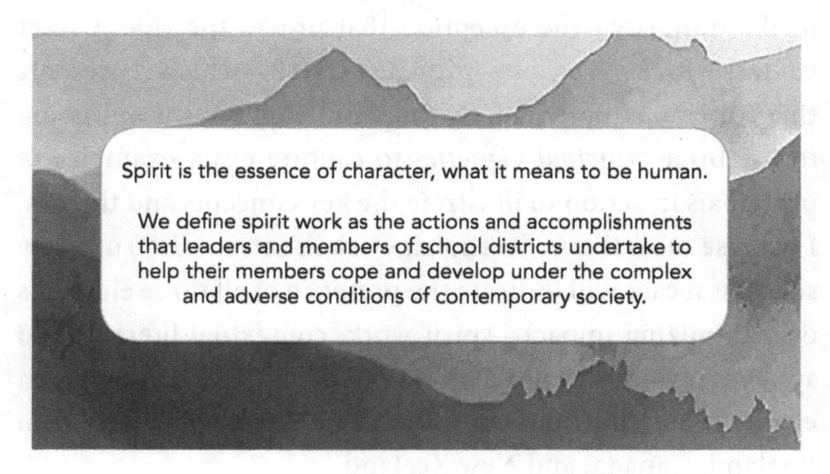

Spirit is the essence of character, what it means to be human.
We define spirit work as the actions and accomplishments that leaders and members of school districts undertake to help their members cope and develop under the complex and adverse conditions of contemporary society.

Margaret Wheatley, one of the modern-day founders of the focus on human spirit, wrote a Foreword to our book in which she said:

> Where do we find the motivation, the energy to resist succumbing to fear and anger, to not be overwhelmed by despair, to stay awake and persevere. We find the answer when we recognize that all that we do as educators, parents, community members, our work is to recognize, value, defend, and protect the human spirit. (Fullan & Edwards, 2022)

So we now have spirit work as the rallying cry for school and school system transformation. It is the first and fundamental key for maximizing the impact of school principals. In one sense schools always had the potential for spirit work. Over the years we have seen this potential in some case studies of communities of high poverty in which leaders and others were able to rescue students from lives of failure. But these individual successes have been very much in the minority—the exception that proves the rule. I want to start with such a case—pre-COVID-19—which represents this enormous potential. Throughout this book I am going to use brief *principal vignettes* to capture exact examples of principals in action to illustrate the key concepts and themes. I will use cases that reflect spirit work in action. (In truth, any successful case will indicate the presence of all three elements of maximizing impact—spirit work, contextual literacy, and systemness—but I will select cases that best exemplify a given element.) In this chapter I report on three vignettes from England, Canada, and New Zealand.

Our first stop is to Northern England. Benjamin Adlard Primary School (Benji). By 2014 Benji was rated by England's inspection agency (OFSTED) as one of the worse schools in the country. It consistently assessed well below standard, eventually ending with the ominous official designation—"in need of special measures." In December 2014, Marie-Claire Bretherton, age 35, was appointed from another successful school in the region as the new head of Benji with the mandate to turn the school around. In this book, I want to capture principals in action; Benji represents a perfect case. I interviewed Bretherton in June 2018, three-and-a-half years into her term, which is the period of turnaround—and is the focus of *the following "Principal Vignette 3.1,"* representing spirit work. Interestingly, I also interviewed Bretherton and her chief assistant, Sam Coy, in July 2022 to update with respect to COVID-19 and to explore their work and relationship with the community, which is part of our system focus. These results are reported in Chapter 5 as *"Principal Vignette 5.1"*. Here we start at the beginning in 2014.

Principal Vignette 3.1: Marie-Clare Bretherton, Benjamin Adlard Primary School, Lincolnshire, England

Benjamin Adlard Primary School serves a highly deprived area in Lincolnshire about 150 miles north of London. Nearly 70% of the pupils are eligible for free school meals; poverty levels are in the bottom 10% nationally; 30% of the pupils have special needs requiring significant additional support; and the school is close to the bottom of the performance tables in the country. Bretherton, coming from a successful school in the region, took over in December 2014. She observed, "I know what I am doing in my own school that works, but I knew that it was never going to be completely translatable to Benjamin Adlard. The context was different, the staff was different, and although the mission and values were the same, the approach needed to be different. I knew a linear strategy wouldn't work."

The only staff change Bretherton made was to hire an assistant principal (Sam Coy) to help her. Here is what she did at the very beginning:

> I interviewed every single member of staff, from cleaner to deputy head, just asking them everything they could tell me about the school and its history. There were so many challenges, they said. They said to me, whatever you think you know, it is not going to work here, we've tried everything. These children just aren't capable of succeeding in school; the challenges they face in life are just too big. I kept saying there is some good stuff here. At my first staff meeting I said you may think I am going to come in and sack you all.

(*Continued*)

That's not what I am going to do. All I ask is that you turn up every day and that you are willing to learn and that's all I need from you; we'll do it together. That was very counter-cultural and a big gamble. You know we didn't lose anybody. All of them stayed. I think the big challenge was the school had been isolated and the teachers within it had been isolated, too. They had no sense of connection with each other, or with schools in the local area.

My rhetoric was "we will do this together." I'm not going to come in as a leader and work in isolation with each of you. We're in this as a team so we've got to bring a kind of challenge to one another and support to one another. There was quite a bit of messaging, and there were times, honestly, that I really didn't know if I actually believed it was possible. But I gave myself a pep talk every day. It took me 20 minutes to drive from my house to the school. Every single day I would rehearse to myself about the school. So you know if you rehearse the positive, you rehearse the possible, you rehearse the vision, and it helps you that there is hope, because I knew that if I didn't do that and once I arrived at school, it would only take about 10 minutes before I would be overwhelmed with hopelessness.

Myself and Sam had a policy. For the first eight weeks we would not give any negative feedback. We literally went on a mission to find anything that we could possibly observe that was good. We knew that as soon as we came in with a hard message pointing out where things were far from good, it would have killed any sense of optimism. We needed to build a sense that there was hope. We had to gently coach, encourage, and nourish, and build a relationship with the team so that in time we would be able to give some really specific and clear feedback about what needed to improve, but needed a relational basis on which to do it, and we needed them to know that they had strengths to build on.

As Marie-Claire and Sam built relationships, they gradually shifted to capacity building:

There was a lot of skilling-up of the workforce, first of all in managing pupils, keeping pupils in class, and creating a culture where pupils' emotional and social needs were met. Sam and I felt we needed to do that first because if we pitched curriculum, pedagogy, and assessment first before teachers felt confident enough to manage the room, they were going to get lost. That was difficult because the accountability pressure from OFSTED was very much demanding we sort out teaching first. Once teachers felt that [they] could keep pupils in class we moved onto curriculum and instruction.

We had to be very careful in terms of who we brought in, making sure that they came in with servant-hearted humility, competence and expertise, definite skills around coaching, and with the aim of building in school capacity. We did a lot of personalizing our approach to each teacher. We focused on which teachers were going to be our quick wins, who could learn quickly and raise the bar about what's possible. I think that some of the teachers who had been in the school the longest were the most difficult to get on board initially, although they became the strongest and most loyal colleagues. At the beginning there was a significant level of cynicism.

(*Continued*)

One teacher, who had actually some strong areas of practice, was particularly reluctant to work with others within the school or outside the school. He was very competent with the children and how to manage them, but he was also a maverick at times. We used a tool that we created called "teacher tracker" with each teacher to identify and monitor specific teacher competencies in terms of instruction and behavior management. Sam and I spent a lot of time in classrooms examining the trends.

The turning point for him was when we said, okay, we'd like you to go and work with the class teacher in Year 5 because you're really strong in competency A, B, and C, and she's got D nailed. Work together. I think he realized that he had something specific to teach someone else, but also something very specific that he could use to refine his own practice further. This also gave them a clear focus. That relationship really began to transform both of them. They were observing each other teach. They were planning stuff together, marking work together, and assessing pupil progress together. They sat eyeball to eyeball and began to really digest their practice.

My big message is that it takes an alliance to improve a school. In the work of the alliance you see the power of the network, the power of peer review, the power of student voice, and the power of collective responsibility. One of the things we did was to invite pupils from other schools to come in and do a pupil-led peer review, to come into the school and tell us what they thought we were missing. Among other things students told us: "Your library is full of books for girls. Where are your books for boys? Your playground is boring. It is all

> concrete. Where is the grass? Where is the green?" So, we brought in students from other schools to work with our students to talk about how they would make our school better, really getting into the detail.

The OFSTED inspection came in June 2016 (one-and-a-half years after Bretherton started):

> Oh, it was the most incredible moment of my life. It really was. We answered the question: it was possible to restore and redeem a school without sweeping it out.
>
> So when I got the chance to tell the staff, I took them to the staff room and everyone was standing around with bated breath. I did a bit of a preamble and then just said, "I didn't need somebody from outside to come and tell me that this is a good school and that you are really good at what you do, but I can now officially tell you that you are good—you are a good school!"
>
> Teachers fell to their knees and wept tears of joy. Some staff described it as a life-changing moment. One teacher in particular said they felt like they could now hold their head up high and talk proudly about who they are and where they work, for the first time in their career.

I chose Ben Adlard school as a spirit work example as it represents the depths of humanity at work. Here was a school that had been stuck for many years in a sea of hopelessness. It took a special kind of leadership to lead the school out of what anyone familiar with the community would have said was a hopeless proposition. This case

(*Continued*)

puts a new light on the question of school turnaround. This is not a matter of raising academic performance (although it did that). Rather, it was, and there is no other way to put it, *spirit work in action that changes the sense of humanity, life chances, and orientation to the world of students, teachers, parents, and community members.*

I asked Bretherton what she had learned about leadership:

> Putting the school improvement bit to one side, it was actually the transformation of humanity that really meant something to me in the school. It restored professional confidence. It's given them life. It's given them hope. It's given them purpose. The school is now oversubscribed. We've got people wanting to come and work here. We've just announced that the school has won the silver award in the Pearson Teaching Awards in the category "School of the Year—Making a Difference" for its work to Transform the Community. I think I've probably underestimated in the past the power of your own sense of vision and hope, and your own mental discipline, and your own belief. That for me was a massive learning curve. Just being able to conjure up in yourself optimism and hope where you are in the face of somebody who tells you or something tells you that it's not possible. What I learned is about the leadership of humanity. It changes the lives of staff, pupils, and parents. It opened my eyes to the role of a leader in the community. I was absolutely terrified by the challenge. I had no idea I could do this. I had no clue. But I believe I've got enough in me to learn how to do it if I go into it with the right kind of attitude.

This marks the end of "Principal Vignette 3.1." We will return to Bretherton, Coy, and Benjamin Adlard in Chapter 5 in another vignette in reference to systemness as we expand on the role of schools as part and parcel of community development under conditions of COVID-19. In the meantime, let's take another example, less dramatic but indicative of spirit work: What does a school do when hit by the massive disruption of the pandemic?

Our second vignette comes from our work in deep learning. Bessborough Elementary School in New Brunswick, Canada, joined our network as part of its district's membership in our NPDL network of schools across several countries (https://www.deep-learning.global/). Our interest here is how the school adjusted to the pandemic. The following vignette is based on an interview conducted by Mag Gardner, one of our senior coordinators.

Principal Vignette 3.2: Nick Mattatal, Bessborough School, East Anglophone District, New Brunswick

The Pivoting Principal

Nick is the principal at Bessborough, a Kindergarten to Grade 8 school with 570 students located in an East Anglophone District, New Brunswick, Canada. In seven years, his school has grown to integrate deep learning at all levels. The community is diverse, with 12–15% in free breakfast daily. Students are from 27 countries with 18 different languages spoken. His secret to leadership?

(*Continued*)

He remarks modestly, "I work with good people, and I just try to make it work for them." Humility is an authentic and central character trait of Nick but that wouldn't be enough to motivate students, staff, and parents to make the shift from traditional to deep learning.

Nick sees his role as a connector. What resources do teachers need to fulfill their deep learning plan? How does their plan dovetail with the school's plan? Teachers don't have the time or the network to make this happen so Nick taps community, district, and other partners for support. For example, when Sally's Grade 7 students were determined to build solar-powered robotic seed sorters for the school's garden, Sally needed support with programming, technical support, mentoring, and funding. Nick reached out to district consultants and also released another teacher for part of the time to co-facilitate with Sally.

Deep learning plans don't always unfold in a linear way. Nick recognizes that it is messy. Everyone in his school community learns that failure is just a part of the learning process. He believes staff and students need to get used to being flexible and get over the need for perfection. As he says, "It's not the end of the world. Nobody's going to die!"

As a principal, Nick is always prepared to pivot. In fact, he expects it. He sees his role as: "Finding ways to make teachers the catalysts. We have developed a 9 criteria model which we use to screen new ideas" (Figure 3.2).

Figure 3.2 9 Pillars: Bessborough Elementary School (Figure provided by Nick Mattatal)

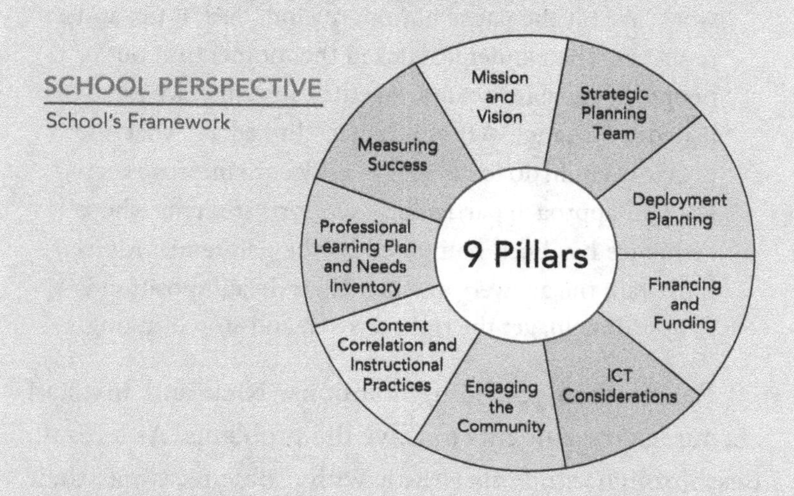

The 9 Pillars model was created by Nick and his colleagues to flesh out some of the details from our deep learning model. They have applied this model to guide the development of several local innovations for which they have videos and photos, including a sweat equity pollinator garden, tiny homes simulation, and robotic seed spreaders, all related to the community that is mostly rural incorporating several farms.

In developing new ideas, the group tries to answer the question and learn from the experience with respect to "What does a good learning project look like." As Nick put it:

(*Continued*)

> I work with good people and learn from them. I try to get rid of the failure factor. Sometimes things don't work. We hit the pause button, rewind, back it up, and re-assess. The pandemic sucked the momentum out of people being able to work together. Recently, we established a "Change Action Center" linked to what the province could do to develop new ideas to improve society. Our approach particularly supports students whose resilience has been hampered by the pandemic. Many kids want the answers quickly. Their default position is to ask for help, get the right answer, and stop thinking.

Rather than providing solutions, Nick and his staff encourage the students to solve the problems. As a result, Bessborough's students wrestle with problems, tweak their plans, and self-evaluate. Kids are now taking the lead. Nick elaborates:

> Kids can nag teachers in a good way. This perseverance allows them to engage in creative and critical thinking. Seeing the kids being excited, and seeing them do innovative things is a great motivator. Kids have huge imaginations. Traditional school kills their imagination.

Once new ideas are on the move Nick tries to leverage the momentum. He observes:

> New teachers are now wanting to transfer in. The principal's role is to help teachers and students come up with a plan, and work towards it. Find a couple of people who are really on board, and have some success. Make it easy for other people to learn from them, and go little further and further to extend their own ideas.

He concludes:

> You are not leading effectively if you are not taking into account other people's mindsets.

Nick is right. The school has cultivated those mindsets and imaginations, and that has built student self-efficacy and leadership. Students are currently using drones to irrigate the school garden. They are saving the bees. They are building tiny green houses to address homelessness, and even devising solutions for their province's stretched health care system.

> This school-wide culture doesn't just pop up overnight. Nick's advice to other school leaders is to "go slow to go fast." Build a few successes, then take another tiny step. He says, "Think of the work as a reverse funnel, it's small at the beginning, then expands." He also sees school implementation as a circuitous drive in the country with winding roads, potholes, and obstacles, but also new discoveries. "It's not as the crow flies."

Bessborough school does not represent the desperate situation that confronted Marie-Clare Bretherton when she arrived at Benjamin Adlard. It is a regular school that had the benefit of deep learning. In terms of spirit work, it had pretty much sorted out its vision as a school in dynamic times that had to adjust to whatever conditions evolved in the environment. It was on the high ground to pivot, always focusing on the needs of students, parents, and teachers. Teachers and students were aware of

(Continued)

and connected to some of the energy-related priorities of the province. The school was aware of the threats (and opportunities) arising from the pandemic. It was the pandemic that gave additional meaning to the energy-related initiatives that the school undertook during this period. They would relate to the concept of spirit work and its growing importance in their situation and in the larger society. They know that school in 2022 is not business as usual.

Time to move to New Zealand where we have other clusters of schools working on deep learning. New Zealand is an interesting place in more ways than one. We have worked in New Zealand off and on for over two decades. The total population is a little over 5 million consisting of about 70% European descent, 17% Māori, and 8% Pasifika (Pacific Islanders). There is an increasingly strong presence of Māori and Pasifika language and cultures in all aspects of the country, especially so in education. There are approximately 2500 schools in the country. There are no local districts with each of the 2500 schools having their own board. There are 10 administrative regions for education. There is a long-standing debate in the country about centralization and decentralization. There is a system of COLs (Communities of Learning) within which each school is expected to be a member (often some three to eight schools). COLs receive funding, appoint a COL coordinator, and interact in relation to government policy and local priorities.

For this vignette we travel to Wānaka School, which is located in the Central Otago Lakes region in the southeast region of the South Island. Because New Zealand is a small country, there is a lot of immediate context: the local community, the COL or clusters, the region, and the national policy and strategy.

Principal Vignette 3.3: Wendy Bamford, Wānaka School, New Zealand

"The Principal Has to Love It to Lead It"

Wendy Bamford of Wānaka School (570 students) in New Zealand knows that passion drives learning. I love her motto and strategy: "The principal has to love it to lead it." When Wendy came to the school in 2005, she notes that she started "just as the NZ curriculum—with key competencies at the front and learning areas at the back—was released—a great time to implement change." She gives her initial impression: "Many of the staff talked of doing things the Wānaka Way, which was led from the top. There was some good work happening in literacy and numeracy, and around learning tools such as habits of mind and graphic organizers, but no real cohesion with the learning, classroom management, and student management." We see this often: good ideas in the curriculum without pathways to bring them to life in the school. The potential for substantial change existed, but was not enabled.

In late 2016, Wendy attended a deep learning lab that we presented. The primary school with 570 students has been on a deep learning journey since 2017. Wendy doesn't hoard this passion to herself, however. She creates space

(*Continued*)

for her teachers to love and lead deep learning school-wide. Today Wānaka is a thriving deep learning school where global competencies are integrated into reporting and parents are deep learners, too.

Here is how she and her team did it:

> Starting with unpacking the 6Cs [character, citizenship, collaboration, communication, creativity, and critical thinking] was the ideal way to start looking at building teacher capability and student agency. I also inherited an experienced DP and two APS who were deep thinkers themselves and were keen to take on change. Being in an old school, bulging at the seams with rapid roll growth, and a new school campus to design and build, served to hasten our journey to a philosophy which would bring about our vision "empowering a community of learners." We moved into our new school in October 2010. By 2016, after suffering through National Standards, we were desperate to get back to the competencies and to bring the joy and wonderment back to what we were doing.

Note Wendy's reference to national standards. The desirable "new competencies" were in the curriculum but layered in were new national standards that turned out to be ad hoc diversions to new learning ("we were desperate to get back to the competencies"). The DL framework with a network of schools, and central resources through NPDL, provided the mechanism for controlling and propelling the agenda.

A network of four schools gathered for an introduction to deep learning. Instead of prescribing a plan about how they would move forward, Wendy opened up leadership opportunities to the whole staff. "You can't be a good principal and lead everything!" she says. Wendy knew exactly what she was looking for. "You want passionate people" so her message was: "If you have a burning desire to lead this, come see me." Sure enough, three enthusiastic teachers stepped up and got started right away. Interest and evidence of deep learning grew quickly. By year two, the school identified mentors to lead and support groups of teachers. It's been growing ever since. This is textbook "Leadership from the Middle."

Wendy knows that cultivating a culture of shared vision, collaboration, and risk taking is a priority. This is all about spirit work. She recognizes that educational trends come and go. With spirit work, you need to stick with it, dedicating time for teachers to practice and reflect together, especially at the beginning. Today Wānaka is a space where teachers work on daily challenges together and share their strengths, passions, and wonderings in a nonthreatening environment. The dialogue moves from the formalized professional learning days to everyday conversations. Wendy says, "You know the culture is thriving when you overhear the talk at the photocopier: teachers may only have two minutes, but they're talking about deep learning."

The deep dive process, first facilitated by New Pedagogies for Deep Learning (NPDL), takes the school deeper. The collaborative appreciative inquiry process affirms teachers are having an impact and helps them

(*Continued*)

pinpoint where they can take their learning next. Recently, they used the deep dive to look at the learning through a parent's perspective. Board members also got involved in a deep dive experience and were "blown away" by the deep learning they witnessed. Even the parents were talking about the global competencies.

Authentic partner involvement is key to the vitality of deep learning. Wānaka has rich examples of parents learning alongside their children. In science, students were studying gears and building go-karts for an under privileged children fundraiser. Parents rolled up their sleeves and helped with the design and supported the students' construction. In another example, students researched earthquakes and emergency responses. They surveyed families about how they might respond in the event of a disaster. This led them to build emergency kits and create instructional posters for their homes. All of the kits were featured in a school-wide showcase of learning.

In another example, students learned that in Lake Wānaka the eels couldn't get past the dams to spawn in the Pacific waters. Students, 6-year-olds, took up the cause and partnered with parents, the district council, and others to promote the establishing eel slides so they could pass through the dams. The Minister of Conservation came to visit the children at school to see their work and supported their promotion for signage about the eels, for tourists, with the local council.

When parents understand and apply the global competencies at home, the learning is extended. As Wendy says, "Students begin living the learning." Wendy describes a 5-year-old who pursued a creative design at home during COVID-19 lockdown. He produced a play, then made a model, then his parents filmed the experience and sent it into the school. At this early age, the student understood and could reflect on his own independent learning.

Wānaka intentionally communicates the global competencies at every opportunity—through newsletters, reporting, and showcases. The school celebrations of learning are well attended by parents. Wendy says, "You can't get into the space because it's so packed. Everyone attends—99% of the parents and extended family come. Last year only one or two parents in each learning space missed it." Parents at Wānaka are so impressed with deep learning that they want to see it continue at the local secondary school. Students return from the secondary school and thank Wendy and her teachers. They say things like, "Thank you. I know how to learn because of you." Educators know that if there is anything that feeds their passions, it's a statement like that.

At Wānaka we see another change lesson come alive. You don't have to get everyone on board at the beginning. Have a good idea, invite participation, make it easy to get involved, support and celebrate the work of students and teachers, involve parents as the learning gets underway. As a principal, love it and lead it but don't take the credit. You cultivate and call upon the deep commitment of teachers and the community.

Spirit Work in the Service of Maximizing Impact

In short, spirit work is the first and foundational key for maximizing impact of school principals during the perils and opportunities of the dynamic decade in which we find ourselves. As we (Fullan & Edwards, 2022) identified in our study of school districts in the United States, spirit work connotes a deeper commitment to the current lives and futures of youth and their futures. Over the past two decades, the meaning of spirit work has become increasingly evident, and the pandemic only compounded it. In our network, people increasingly see spirit work as foundational to the *humanity paradigm*. It seems like an abstract concept, but in a pandemic-ridden world people of all ages readily grasp it. Recall our official definition (Fullan & Edwards, 2022):

> Spirit is the essence of character—what it means to be human. We define spirit work as the actions and accomplishments that leaders and members of school districts undertake to help their members cope and develop under the complex and adverse conditions of contemporary society. (p. 13)

It is the first of the new three keys for school principals.

A second new key that we have recently worked out goes by the name of *contextual literacy*. It is powerful; it is local; it generates specificity in the quest for system change. Most of all, understanding and improving context are at the heart of success. It is time to step into this rich new territory of daily life in increasingly conflictful difficult times.

CHAPTER FOUR
Contextual Literacy: The Second Key for Maximizing Impact

CHAPTER · FOUR

Contextual Literacy: The Second Key for Maximizing Impact

As is often the case when one is working with practitioners solving big problems, such as how to move forward to improve whole systems, one encounters new ideas that lead to more precise language. When I was writing *Nuance* (Fullan, 2019), I was grappling with Leonardo da Vinci's way of working. He was "getting at the experience of others as a means of understanding them" (see Fullan, 2019, p. 114, and the magnificent biography of Leonardo by Walter Isaacson, 2017). Basically, contextual literacy is knowledge, understanding, and care about the setting in which you are leading. It is deep empathy on the part of leaders for the people and their circumstances of life.

As I contemplated what Leonardo was getting at and what we were facing in our work with local systems, I realized that effective leaders are especially attuned to *context*. As I put it in 2019, "Empathy for context is an essential requirement for making change with the people who live in the context every day" (Fullan, 2019, p. 114). Although I didn't use the full concept at the time, it became a short and inevitable route to conclude that effective leaders need and have to become experts in *contextual literacy*. This is the second key for maximizing the effectiveness of the principal.

The identification of contextual literacy led to a slew of insights about change. Every time you change jobs you become to a certain extent "de-skilled" (since you can't possibly understand all aspects of a new culture upon arrival). Every time the environment substantially changes (such as the pandemic) we *all* become to a degree less skilled in dealing with the new setting. We need to be, as Martin and Osberg (2015) observed, both experts and apprentices. Some of us know some things, and others know different things. We all have something to learn as the world changes. In the end, a premium leadership skill involves becoming contextually literate with respect to the cultures in which we work. In this sense, there is nothing more deflating than for a leader to pretend they know more about a given culture than they do (sometimes called the *impostor syndrome*).

Contextual literacy gives all of us a license to be lead learners and followers. In the context of this book, it means that principals have to be role models in contextual literacy and related continual learning therein, as they foster the same qualities in others. Of course, sometimes the current context can be stagnant—better to know and understand this (and even appreciate its subtle strengths than to be caught unaware). Marie-Claire Bretherton and her chief assistant, Sam Coy, showed great wisdom when they decided to spend eight weeks at the beginning of their tenure to observe and get to know the staff at Ben Adlard prior to initiating any action with them (see Chapter 3).

Before delving into our three vignettes in this chapter, I want to consider the bigger picture in relation to the principal's potential role as a proactive contextually literate and involved leader.

The Bigger Picture

Figure 4.1 displays the principals' potential contextual roles in reference to district culture (Fullan, Spillane, & Fullan, 2022).

Figure 4.1 Connected Autonomy

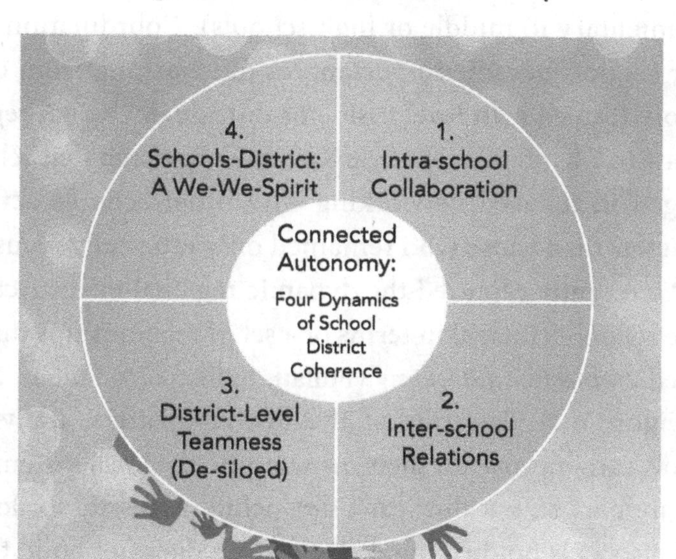

In relation to the principal's potential roles, I start with perspective one—intra-school collaboration—where I include school–parent–community relations. The principal's role is to help orchestrate rapport and focus within the local school and its community. Ideally this is spirit work in action, which we took up in the previous chapter with two case examples (England and New Brunswick). The two principals—Marie-Claire and Nick—stimulated and enabled productive learning and community building. All the principal vignettes across the chapters will encompass this internal to the school-community role.

As schools evolved over the past century, districts or local authorities became a significant part of the immediate context of schools. These days, schools have potentially some new relations with other schools in the region, especially feeder schools (students coming from prekindergarten to elementary or elementary to middle or high schools). Coordination with other schools became important, as did learning from other schools at one's own level inside or outside one's own region. We saw in Chapter 2 from Lyle Kirtman's research that schools engaged in focused networking with other schools actually did better than those who remained only internally focused.

We recently captured the dynamic regional or district role of the school principal in terms of a set of relationships that we labeled *connected autonomy* (Fullan, Spillane, & Fullan, 2022; see Figure 4.1). The role of the district matters. Individual schools can improve on their own despite the local system that they are part of, but they can't *stay* being successful for long if their district is not helping. If the district does not build teams within its level and fails to develop a we-we spirit in the district, it will be difficult to become effective on an ongoing basis. Thus, school principals for example must become knowledgeable about all four quadrants in Figure 4.1 because that is the local context within which they work.

In Chapter 5 we will take up some strategies for success even if the system you are in is less than helpful, but for the time being let's agree that the principal must tend to all four quadrants in Figure 4.1. They must, in other words, become contextually literate of a multifaceted situation. Thus, contextually literate means having empathy for, understanding of, and positive relationships with your immediate social and political environment. I have said that such an orientation is essential with respect to your own school and community. See for example, the Ben Adlard case from Chapter 3 (internal to the school) and Chapter 5 (vis-à-vis the community).

The lesson here is to be a learner at all times while paying careful attention to the culture in which you work. Consider what you can learn from others as well as what you might have to offer. Connected autonomy contains nuances. Healthy environments free up both individuals and groups to take action. Hierarchical power is recognized with formal leaders working on their listening skills and participating as learners. The system uses its power to help people stand up as both autonomous and willingly connected.

In this chapter, I present three vignettes of principals steeped in contextual literacy.

Principal Vignette 4.1 (adapted from Ikler, 2021a): Michelle Pinchot, Heritage Elementary School, Garden Grove District, Anaheim (see Fullan & Pinchot, 2018)

Our team had worked with Garden Grove Unified School District in Anaheim, California, where the district became very successful in increasing student learning in a high-poverty, diverse district. One of these schools was K3 Peters, a very large early learning school. The principal was Michelle Pinchot, whose school success we had filmed. In summer 2016, Michelle was transferred to another large school within the district, Heritage Elementary, that was somewhat stagnant. Michelle and I came to the following agreement: let's see what it would take to turn around Heritage to become a solid-performing school. I would only act as a periodic monitor. Every few months from

(*Continued*)

summer 2016 to fall 2017 (a total of four occasions) I sent Michelle an email asking the following questions:

- What was Heritage like when you arrived?
- What was your plan in the first year?
- How was that plan unfolding at the end of year one?
- What were your strategies in year two?
- What progress is being made in year two? What's next?

I knew if Heritage was to be successful in short order, it would have to be a matter of joint determination between Michelle and the staff. The school did in fact become a fast success, and we published the story in a special issue of *Educational Leadership* on the theme "Leading the Energized School" (Fullan & Pinchot, 2018).

By the second year the school increased literacy and math scores as measured by the state test in California. Garden Grove, the district, conducts an annual climate survey that is based on the criteria of an effective learning environment. At Heritage there were dramatic improvements comparing 2016 to 2018. Figure 4.2 displays the results.

These "changes in culture" are stunning given that they occurred in barely more than two years. How did Pinchot and the staff have such an impact in such a short time period? The answer is that the principal engaged the staff in focused two-way interaction on many interrelated fronts. Here are a half-dozen examples of the leadership strategies that were employed:

Figure 4.2 Heritage Staff Responses, 2016–2018

	2016	2017	2018
Students feel safe at school	71%	94%	94%
Site leadership fosters professional growth and feedback	30%	86%	100%
This school promotes trust and collegiality among staff	68%	88%	100%
This school has a safe environment for giving peer-to-peer feedback	44%	93%	100%
Students ask questions when they don't understand	33%	71%	86%

1. Establishing multiple permanent teams led by teachers that had clearly defined responsibilities
2. Providing a variety of specific teacher professional development sessions with clear expectations and support
3. Developing a school-wide behavioral plan with strong involvement by student, teacher, and parent groups
4. Using instructional rounds to collect data on practices including celebrating implementation of student learning
5. Purchasing digital devices and establishing a new media center
6. As the principal, being highly visible in teacher-led teams and in classrooms in weekly visits while being nonjudgmental, participating as a learner

Pinchot also benefited from having a focused and supportive district much like Ottawa Catholic (as we will see later in this chapter), which helped coordinate, invest in, and support the work at the school level. In such systems, district-school development is also a joint effort.

(*Continued*)

We know from other work and from research that principals who participate as learners, with teachers focusing on teacher leadership for improving pedagogy, have the greatest impact. These principals use the group to change the group; they influence student learning indirectly, but nonetheless explicitly. Their nuance is changing the culture of the school as the powerful foundation for changing the foundation of ongoing learning. When leaders like Pinchot self-consciously lead in this way, they get a feel for this method, knowing when to push or hold back; they respond to and cultivate momentum. They build powerful collaborative cultures over four or five years to the point where they become more dispensable because the school has collaborative leaders who can carry on after the original leaders leave.

There is more from Pinchot. My colleague Jeff Ikler interviewed Pinchot as part of his *Getting Unstuck* leadership change series in an episode titled "Unleashing the Power of a Team of Teacher Leaders" (2021a). I have paraphrased here the key points from the 12-minute interview (to listen to the podcast, see Ikler, 2021). We start with the scene I just described. Michelle got transferred from an elementary school named K-3 Peters in the Garden Grove Unified School District. I had helped Michelle at K-3 Peters where she worked with the staff to develop a highly effective school. Her goal at K-3 Peters, which she achieved over a five-year period, was to obtain strong and measurable success that could continue beyond her tenure. This was an explicit goal: Michelle told me the year before she ended up being transferred, "I wanted the staff, students, and community to become so successful through their efforts that they would reach a point that they could carry on very well, and perhaps even better, if I departed" (personal interview, 2014). Six months later she was transferred to Heritage Elementary School with a mandate bring new life to the school and community.

I think one of the most difficult leadership feats for leaders is to move from one highly successful situation where they have been at the helm to a new situation where they are expected to repeat the high performance. My guess is that the failure rate is at least 50%. The reason is that you can make very few accurate assumptions about the new context if you have not been in the situation (i.e., your contextual literacy is initially weak). What looks obvious (low morale, poor results, bad communication, and the like) are only symptoms. What they hide is the nuance of local personalities, stories, and history peculiar to that particular group. Success, if it is to happen, depends on the ability of the newcomer's skill and commitment to becoming "contextually literate." Michelle Pinchot is brilliant at this. To know when to hold back; when to be assertive; when to be patient; when to accelerate; when to recognize that the best success comes from the group are all capacities that are associated with contextually literate leaders.

(*Continued*)

Let's examine in her own words from the Ikler interview, what Pinchot has to say about stepping into a leadership role with a mandate to help bring about major change in the culture. Michelle starts the interview:

> I'll never forget the opening staff meeting. There is so much preparation, you know, to set the tone for the year, not knowing anyone. We had done a survey prior to my arrival, and I put up a slide that showed only 50% of the staff were proud to work here. That is a telling piece of data for a new principal, and I was thinking that we have quite a task. It says a lot about transparency—I put it on the screen noting that "this is the elephant in the room." And it kind of hushed the room. And I said the goal for me is to turn this into 100% who are proud to be part of this school community. That's where we started. Academic performance, and the suspension rates had been working against the school for a very long time. It was no one's fault but what could the focus be to turn things around? After years of little improvement, people were used to not feeling successful. I could feel that with the teachers, the students, the classified staff. This actually fueled my fire—the challenge, the change that would be needed. It was incredible in a sense to be part of this feeling of heaviness. This wasn't a group of people that didn't want to do well. They wanted to be better but had no idea about where and how do we start. They are craving a pathway out. I loved being part of the leading of that. So, yes, where do you start?
>
> There was a group of people who wanted to do something. I remember our first year. Building relationships

for trust is so crucial in these moments because they have to believe in you. They have to trust what you say you will do, and that there will be follow through. We had to do so much listening. My assistant, Chris, and I had to do so much listening. We would just tag team: you talk with this group; I'll talk with that group. We unpacked what we gathered. I know that this sounds odd but the intuition of when to push and when to pull is crucial. We knew we had a good group of teachers. We needed to find out what their gifts were. It was our job to figure out what can each person bring to the task. They needed very defined roles and responsibilities for leadership teams. We needed them to own "it"—for the work to be theirs not ours. Of course, as an outsider you can come in and go through the data and provide a checklist of ideas to fix the problem, but if you can't empower others to do something it will never be theirs. If you empower others, it will always be sustainable when you leave. Will the culture and climate that you created together continue after you leave? It needs to be theirs because they have done the research and the learning.

When it is happening, the energy that is being created, and is happening, you can't really put into words. Sometimes you have to stand by and observe and say, "wow, look at that." What they are able to do sometimes is fantastic. They became an enthusiastic group, once they had permission. Once we knew the areas that needed to be fixed—they needed to figure out how to do it.

(*Continued*)

> From the beginning, I could figure out who wanted to act—"let's do it" and who wanted to step back and wait and see what would happen. We started very small to get big [quoting my (Fullan's) work, Michelle said: go slow to go fast, use the group to move the group, etc.]. A lot of the times we are in a hurry and we don't celebrate the small things. And boy oh boy, we celebrated every achievement whether it is small or large, whether we met or exceeded a benchmark. You have to celebrate every step of the way. It helps to create a sense of team and ownership. And it helps those who are sitting and waiting. It becomes infectious. It's kind of hard to be the one sitting in the back of the room with your arms crossed when everyone else is celebrating.

Jeff then asked Michelle whether academic performance was the main measure of success. Michelle replied, "No, probably the opposite. We didn't even consider academics until we could understand the school community, and when a school is labeled at risk, what does that even mean? Of course, its academic but that's usually a result of other things. Why aren't they able to achieve academically? Most definitely we had to look at socioemotional learning, enrichment, after school programs, so many different things in order to get to academic. Why were attendance rates low; why were suspension rates high?"

In wrapping up Michelle said:

> I thrive on mentoring others to be their best. I like to try and figure out what each person can bring to the table and pull the best out of them. We may have

> state mandates, district recommendations, but how we get there is our own doing. How we encourage and develop others that is not part of any mandate anywhere. The next phase is preparing the school to eventually be without me in the front.

Finally, Jeff asked what advice Michelle might have for young principals who were starting out. Her response:

> Build relationships, take the time to get to know your people, really taking time to know who they are as people, and sit back your first year, take a deep breath to observe what is happening, what is working, and what's not. And listen, listen, listen.

All aspects of life at Heritage improved in a short period of time: morale, suspension rates, engagement of staff, students and community, academic grades, and so on. Leading with contextual literacy is by definition a comprehensive strategy.

In this next vignette—Ottawa Catholic School Board (OCSB)—we take a whole district of 83 schools to first examine one principal, and then the district as a whole.

Ottawa Catholic School Board consists of 83 schools with some 43,000 students. Ever aware of cultivating system change with a "go slow to go fast" motif, Director (Superintendent) of Education Denise Andre and Deputy Director Tom D'Amico developed a plan with us whereby 7 of the 83 schools (one in each of the geographic areas of the city of Ottawa) decided to be the first cohort. It was clearly understood that all other schools would join in. In year two, a further eight schools were added; in year three the remaining 68 schools joined. Going slow for them meant that the entire system was involved within 24 months. A year later Tom D'Amico was appointed director as Denise Andre retired.

Contextual literacy in this case example means the entire district. I will take it up in two steps: first by focusing on one principal at the school level where his context is the district; and then by taking the entire district as the context.

Principal Vignette 4.2: JP Cloutier, Notre Dame High School, Ottawa Catholic School Board (OCSB)

This vignette is an example of how the district can shape in a positive way the role of a principal; and how in turn the principal sees district success as part and parcel of school success.

JP Cloutier has been an educator with the Ottawa Catholic School Board (OCSB) for over 20 years.

The role of the principal requires astute political awareness and an understanding of the global context that the school is part of. After building his network of colleagues at two different high schools as vice principal, JP was promoted to the role of principal in 2020. Notre Dame is a Grade 7–12 school of about 700 students. The school is designated as a children support school by the board and is part of the Ontario Ministry of Education Urban Priority high school initiative. This initiative provides support for students to improve literacy and numeracy skills while connecting with their community and learning valuable leadership skills that might not otherwise be available to them. Through a partnership with Dovercourt Recreation Center, the school offers free programming at the end of the school day from 3:00 to 5:30 p.m. Every day students can sign up for any number of student services, such as tutoring, swimming, music, drama, and leadership.

JP's focus on learning partnerships has helped Notre Dame connect students to their individual passions both inside and outside the classroom. The school has partnered with technology company Ciena, to participate in Ciena solutions challenge by Digital Promise. Using relationship-building strategies, students become partners in the learning environment. Students have opportunities to select their own learning activities and have a voice in their learning. Leveraging technology to make a difference in the lives of others has helped to turn students into creators where they could impact their school and local community. The pride and excitement of student learning is highlighted by JP when he intentionally celebrates innovative teachers on his staff. The Ciena solutions challenge is a practical example of deep learning in action as students express pride in their learning and how they use technology to make a difference.

In response to the Black Lives Matter (BLM) movement, students at Notre Dame wanted to make a difference. Four students, two of whom were Black, began to

(*Continued*)

discuss the idea that the BLM designation should become part of the school uniform. Several things happened at pretty much the same time. The BLM shirt was designed and approved by the student council as part of the school uniform. The Black Students' Association (BSA) was created, and the campaign moved from the student council to the BSA. The idea was supported by JP as principal, reflecting an open process run by students and clearly seen as a school-wide endeavor. The whole matter was quickly endorsed by the whole school and reported in the Ottawa news channel under the banner headline: Ottawa high schools students create Black Lives Matter shirts that can be worn at school" (March 8, 2021). The funds generated from the sale of shirts was donated to the Agnes Zabali Boys and Girls Club in Uganda, a club created by a former Notre Dame high school graduate, Jimmy Sebulime. JP created opportunities for the students to share their experience with the media, at a board meeting, and with other schools across the city. This learning activity and experience happened outside the class and has given students true agency in making a difference in their local school, across their community, and across borders. The students from the BSA shared their experience with other school BSAs and then with the director of education as part of the Black Student Advisory Council. This resulted in board-wide changes to the school uniform and dress code policies. This is learning that sticks, and the students will never forget the impact they had.

I asked JP to reflect on the definition of the modern principal in 2022, and this was his response:

> Principals are professional collaborators. In my view, the main role of the principal today is to lead change by implementing the board's vision while responding to the specific needs of the school community. To drive change, we build community and capacity by leading from the middle.
>
> We have a responsibility to both follow and lead as we collaborate with system leaders and consultants who provide guidance and hear our concerns; principals from other schools as we share ideas and resources; staff members who learn alongside us and share their views; families and community partners; and, most importantly, the students who we serve. These relationships are central to the principal's role as community builder.
>
> We care about our school communities and position ourselves as learners. As we build relationships and look for opportunities for staff and students, we develop a greater understanding of how we can contribute to both the school and the system at large. With this understanding, we are able to respond to the needs of our communities and to leverage our position to support student learning.
>
> Looking forward, a widespread desire among educators for a better normal makes this a very exciting time

(*Continued*)

> to be a principal. While the OCSB strategic commitments and the deep learning framework have been a focus for many years, the challenges presented in recent years have highlighted their necessity if we want our students to seize the future, however uncertain it might be.
>
> Equity drives our actions in education, and principals must continue to be allies for staff, students, and school communities. Principals are in a position to support staff members both in their learning and in their efforts to provide students the means to achieve. Most importantly, in the pursuit of equitable outcomes for each student in our system, principals must continue to take a learning role.
>
> I am inspired by both the students demonstrating global citizenship right now and the innovative educators providing them with the opportunities to do so. The students and staff working together towards change are setting a strong example for what is possible. There is much to be gained by taking this moment to make a difference rather than waiting for tomorrow. (personal interview August, 2022)

Notice that JP explicitly sees his role as "contributing to the school and the system at large." As a principal JP keeps relationships front and center with everything he does. He is instrumental in building learning partnerships and expanding the learning environment beyond the classroom. He recognizes the importance of the humane use of technology to make a difference in the world. In terms of student voice, he has used his power and privilege to move from tokenism to true student agency. Leading in a complex environment requires a network of support and JP used his own network of leaders from across the system, and the community partnerships as ways of finding new solutions to challenges in the school.

District Context

With Ottawa we have the opportunity to consider the relationship between the school and the district levels. I see this as a matter of connected autonomy between the levels. The district develops with schools the strategic framework. In the case of OCSB three strategic commitments (Be Community, Be Innovative, Be Well) formed the framework jointly produced by the schools and the board. Note that this threefold framework was developed in 2018 prior to COVID-19 and renewed by the board in 2022. They did not place academic achievement as a top priority (even though they do very well in that respect). For them, well-being and learning together are the guiding principles. This action by the district is significant because it was done *before the pandemic*. The board highlighted well-being as encompassing academic success—a decision that put them in good stead when the emotional pressures of the pandemic amassed over the past three years. When the latter happened, that district already had the instinct and capacity to provide well-being support

(*Continued*)

in the context of the 6 global competencies (character, citizenship, collaboration, communication, creativity, and critical thinking).

Another critical feature of the district is its awareness and cultivation of contextual literacy within and across the school and system levels. The relative autonomy of school principals in their own community is valued, along with many opportunities to interact with peers and the central administration. On more than one occasion Tom D'Amico has mentioned to me that most of the best ideas that he gets are from their interactions with schools and communities.

The following is how Tom described the principal's role (personal communication, August, 2022):

> The Ottawa Catholic School Board (OCSB) recognizes the incredible challenges and complexities of being a school principal. Relationship building continues to be a key priority for administrators to meet with success. The board's strategic commitments are Be Community, Be Innovative, and Be Well.

The interconnectedness of the school to its local community and the global political realities are new challenges and opportunities for school principals. Principals in today's schools must understand the realities of past miscarriages of justice such as the impact of residential schools on multiple generations of indigenous peoples. There are new opportunities for indigenous ways of teaching and learning partnerships with community elders, along with school improvement plans that include a focus on truth and reconciliation.

Today's principal needs to understand their privileged position and the power that comes with the role. Principals need to learn and grow in all areas of equity work with their staff and students. Providing a true voice to students and staff from traditionally marginalized communities needs to be part of today's principal skill set. There are many opportunities to move from tokenism to authentic agency when the principal focuses on listening and creates school and community learning partnerships. Today's principal needs to use their network to create expanded learning partnerships between classes, across grades, across schools, and across district boundaries and borders.

Effective principals have always been lifelong learners; however, today's principal needs to spend time reflecting inwardly to have a better understanding of the biases that they may bring with them into their role. In the OCSB, all aspiring leaders must demonstrate an understanding of how deep learning is a needed reform in education. All administrators in the OCSB taking part on interview teams must have first completed an anti-bias interviewing course.

A previous cohort of principals needed to recognize the importance of using technology and moving from substitution to redefinition for transformation. Today's principals need to focus on how technology can be used

(*Continued*)

to level the playing field for those traditionally marginalized, and provide equity of access to all in their school community. Most importantly, today's principal needs to focus on the humane use of technology.

As the school community, staff, and students become more diverse, the role of the principal continues to evolve. School principals need to be creative to ensure that their school and curriculum is representative of those that it serves. A focus on learning partnerships and building community is one way for school principals to grow in this area. Principals must continue to focus on pedagogical practices and must "use the group to move the group." What has changed for today's principal is that the key leaders to move the group may come from the staff, from students, or from the community.

The complexities of the school and competing community demands, also dictate that principals need to build their conflict resolution skills. Dealing with conflict needs to focus on both student conflict and adult conflict in today's school environment.

As schools transform to learning environments that focus on both academic achievement and staff and student well-being, the role of the principal must also change. The traditional view of the principal as the charismatic leader that can do it all must change. The OCSB has adopted a view that promotes distributed leadership and using the talents amongst all the staff, the students, and the community, as the leadership model that is positioned to deal with the complexities of today's school environment.

In sum, for OCSB the role of the principal is no longer to prepare students for an unpredictable job market but rather to help staff and students make a difference in their world today and build a better future together.

Last, in this chapter, I take up a third strong example of contextual literacy—this time in Australia. Clearly by definition each context is different. But there are common elements—in particular the three keys. Another common feature I hold to is the way all these principals adhere to connected autonomy. They are in charge of their schools, but they also recognize and embrace the necessity to relate to other schools laterally and to the vertical system in which they operate. Esme Capp, the principal of Princes Hill Primary School in Melbourne, Australia, mobilizes the staff and the community to develop a shared focus and to continuously expand new possibilities into the future.

Principal Vignette 4.3: Esme Capp, Princes Hill Primary School, Melbourne, Australia

The "provoking possibilities" principal

At the school in Melbourne, Australia, where *everyone is a researcher,* Esme Capp is the principal at Princes Hill Primary School (PHPS), a foundation (Grade 1) to Year 6 school with an enrollment of 360 students and

(*Continued*)

26 staff members in inner-city Melbourne. The doors at Princes Hill Primary School opened in 1889, but under Esme's leadership, since 2009 it is firmly positioned in the twenty-first century and beyond. The school has created a new grammar of schooling, informed by research with an unwavering focus on learners engaged in meaningful authentic learning experiences.

Linking research and practice, Esme led transformation in pedagogical practice, organizational structures, and physical environments. Developing a unique community of practice, Esme sees research as a way of thinking about teaching and learning and supports her staff to be "Teachers as researchers" developing an ever-evolving shared practice. Esme sees her role as "*provoking possibilities*" for staff, students, and the community.

Esme says, "Leading transformation takes courage, you need to be a risk taker and you may not be popular! Not everyone will be on board initially but begin with some core staff who can see the vision early and support them to embed the ideas. Your best advocates will be the children—they will win over the community and often the reticent teachers."

Esme is passionate about fostering a learning culture that is visible, positive, and owned by the community. Esme partnered with the whole community to articulate their shared purpose and establish school values and beliefs.

Esme says, "At Princes Hill Primary School, we put children's learning first. Each child is unique, with their own strengths, challenges, and potential. Our role as educators is to nurture in children their desire for life-long learning and their capacity to exercise judgement and responsibility in a rapidly changing world, that they are already helping to shape" (Figure 4.3).

Figure 4.3 Princes Hill Values

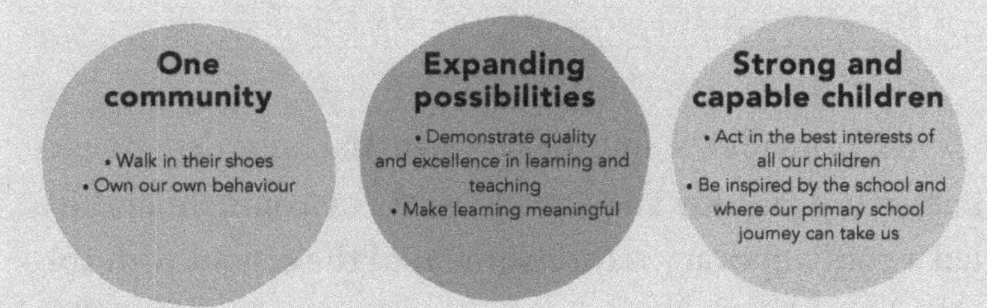

Our VALUES
ABOVE ALL, WE BELIEVE IN...
One community
• Walk in their shoes
• Own our own behaviour
Expanding possibilities
• Demonstrate quality and excellence in learning and teaching
• Make learning meaningful
Strong and capable children
• Act in the best interests of all our children
• Be inspired by the school and where our primary school journey can take us

Esme says, "We live by our learning principles." These principles were developed collaboratively with staff, considering how they believed children learn; the list now underpins the school's approach and is the foundation in all decision-making in the school.

The learning principles (Figure 4.4) and accompanying philosophical and pedagogical framework support staff to align their practices, structures, and learning space, providing an anchor for staff to design learning opportunities and ensuring consistency in pedagogy.

(*Continued*)

Figure 4.4 Principles of Learning

- We develop motives to learn through positioning ourselves within social situations.
- We learn through the unity of emotions and intellect.
- We learn through critical engagement in complex, purposeful contexts where relevant connections are made to our world.
- We learn through consciousness of thought where we reconfigure pre-existing understandings and concepts.
- We learn through active participation in the many forms of expression.

As principal, Esme believes in the interdependence between pedagogy and the physical environment and has led a contemporary refurbishment of the school with specialist architectural designer Mary Featherston AM. The school has established separate neighborhoods (home bases) for five learning communities. To support the wide range of concurrent social-learning experiences essential to collective inquiry, the spatial organization of each neighborhood comprises an assemblage of discrete settings with visual connection and clear circulation paths between all settings (Figure 4.5). These settings are relatively permanent rather than totally flexible. Each is designed to attract, engage, and sustain engagement by providing "cues" for use and by placing relevant resources at point of use. Settings include: focused discussions, studio lab spaces, large active groups, construction/making, quiet reading and relaxing, and multimedia production.

Figure 4.5 Home-Based Floor Plan

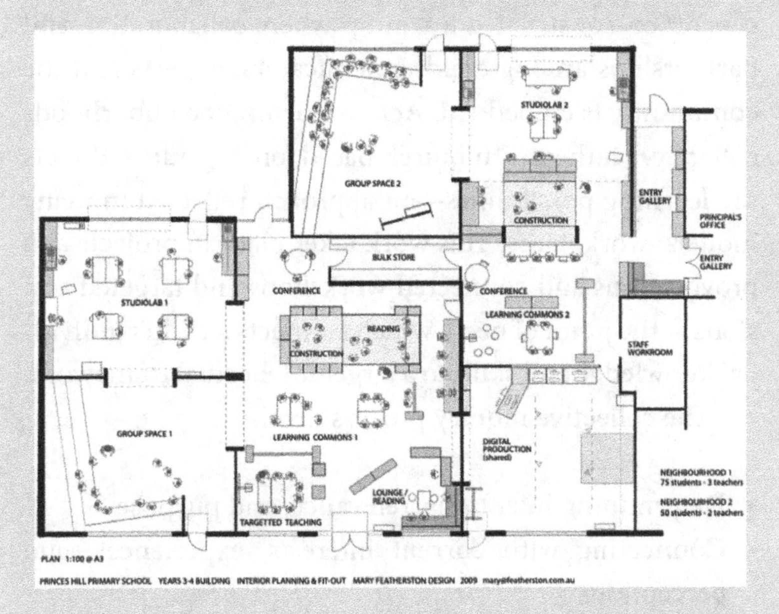

The result is beautiful, enticing, open-aired living and learning spaces that promote focused and shared relationships—learning that has simultaneously a close-knit family feel with an expansive identity to the school as a whole.

All of this is part of a holistic approach to learning and development of the individual connected to the culture. As Esme puts it, "We know that children who actively

(*Continued*)

participate in their learning, learn more." So creating a culture based on collective inquiry, a comprehensive approach to learning and development of the individual and the culture, guides her thinking. Esme has led a process of "co-constructed learning" where collaboration and partnerships among children, educators, experts and the community is embedded. Across learning neighborhoods collective authentic inquires based on big ideas directs the learning possibilities—an approach reflected in many modern workplaces. This work takes place in projects and provocations and connected workshops and targeted sessions at the point of need, which connects a child's individual knowledge and skills to a larger intellectual framework.

The collective inquiry process involves:

- Determining intentions, relevance, and purpose
- Connecting with current interests, experiences, and perceptions
- Expanding possibilities including knowledge, skills, and understandings
- Applying an authentic meaningful context
- Communicating the collective endeavor
- Reflecting on the experience and development of the participants and the community

Collective inquiry develops academic learning alongside the skills to think critically and creatively, to collaborate and communicate, to be active citizens, and to build character. Collective inquiries can be initiated, and intentions developed, by any community member.

Making the learning visible through documentation is important in informing the direction of an inquiry as well as sharing the completed projects. When you have time visit the website to step inside learning at Princes Hill.

A collective inquiry in year one was, What is Play? The teachers thought that by exploring a subject children were experts in, they would be able to uncover the complexities of culture. The children explored different play contexts, including a retirement village—games from 50 years ago; another primary school—how our peers affect how and what we play; traditional indigenous games—how place affects play. The children shared their research at a film festival. Discussions led to a further authentic project designing and making toys for refugee children. A message to a refugee child reads, "I think you are always free if you are a person with hope."

Assessment is a window into both learner development and teacher practice. Esme and her staff value teacher judgments. The meaningful collection of evidence of the development of the student as a writer, artist, reader, mathematician, citizen, or scientist are valuable—it is not just a score that matters. Empowering student curiosity and agency through engagement in deep, meaningful learning experiences is a feature of Princes Hill. Assessment is not based on a deficit model but rather a diverse strengths-based approach leveraging portfolios and other rich qualitative assessments. Esme says current

(*Continued*)

research is engaged with "What is the image of the ideal graduate from PHPS?" and how can new metrics be created and validated to measure what is valued.

Esme's reflections on successful transformation reveal a consistent, multifaceted focus that has been challenging but has supported teachers, students, and the community to "provoke the possibilities." The learners and learning are the focus. One parent has commented, "The children at this school speak of the school and their experience of learning here, with fervent passion." As you wander through the school, learners are engaged and purposeful. Princes Hill is a learning community you would want your child or grandchild to be part of.

Finally, we note that as with all our successful principals in this book, Esme combines internal development and coherence with external partnerships that increase innovation and efficacy. PHPS connects the school with other like-minded educational settings through collective research. For example, it is one of 35 schools throughout Australia that is working in partnership with Melbourne University on a major policy initiative called New Metrics for Success—a high-profile endeavor that seeks to replace standardized tests with assessment more conducive to learning and to the success of graduating students. The school also is involved in the Reggio Children movement through contributing to and participating in the Reggio Emilia Australia Information Exchange. These examples reflect what we call going outside to get better inside while simultaneously making a contribution to the broader system.

PHPS is also proudly a Victorian government school. In our system work, we see schools as proactive contributors to, and consumers of, government policy. Practice is aligned to the Department of Education (DET) initiatives and policy. Examination with staff of the research behind new policies is a catalyst for examining practice and using this analysis to provoke reflection and professional learning. Esme supports DET in developing new initiatives such as Amplify, empowering students through voice, agency, and leadership, and leadership and principal development programs. She also engages the school in participation in DET research projects, including New Pedagogies for Deep Learning. A regional network enables collaborations with local schools through professional learning communities with a focus on practice development aligned to DET initiatives. In 2020, Esme won the DET Principal of the Year for excellence in supporting the system and effective implementation of DET initiatives. This is the fine balance that I have referred to elsewhere as, *We want governments to like what schools are doing, but not to run them.* Connected autonomy at its best.

Finally, we note the congruence with the Victorian government's policy framework (in Australia, like Canada, education is the legal responsibility of the individual states and provinces). Policy and practice are in sync with schools having focused connected autonomy.

I will return to the policy context in the final chapter. I stress here that there is a halting move on the part of governments (such as Victoria) to replace individual academic performance in high-stakes tests with learning and well-being and the factors that support it such as the five in Figure 4.6.

Figure 4.6 Framework for Improving Student Outcomes (FIS0)

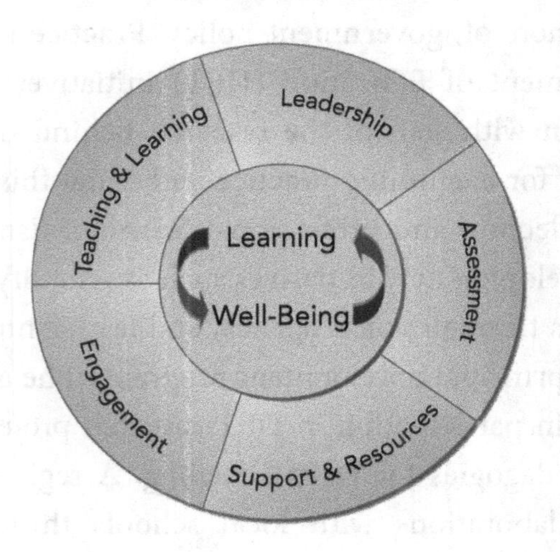

Conclusion

In a subsequent meeting with external guests at Notre Dame High School, one of the students who previously was on the verge of dropping out was filmed expounding to guests how much he now loved school, and the sense of community within it. One of our staff said as an aside to JP the principal: "You should use this film clip to promote the school". The principal, JP replied: "No, I want to show it to his mother! Spirit work and contextual literacy to the core! All eight principal vignettes across chapters show proactive leaders at the school and district levels acting as semi- independent agents plugged into bigger systems. They show the strength of the bottom and the middle in the quest for system change. A reminder that although these middle chapters (Chapters 3–5) focus on each of the three keys, no effective system addresses one key at a time.

We have one more stop before we complete the ring of keys. When we turn to systemness, it gets more complex—and more exciting.

CHAPTER ONE
The Three Keys: Picking Up the Pieces

CHAPTER TWO
A Long Time Coming

CHAPTER THREE
Spirit Work: The First Key for Maximizing Impact

CHAPTER FOUR
Contextual Literacy: The Second Key for Maximizing Impact

CHAPTER FIVE
Systemness in Action: The Third Key for Maximizing Impact

CHAPTER SIX
Future Making

CHAPTER · FIVE

Systemness in Action: The Third Key for Maximizing Impact

Systemness of course is a very elusive concept. I define it as practically as possible. It is about oneself—you as a reader—and all relevant things outside you. It is to be *aware, concerned about,* and *involved in* things that are beyond you but in some ways affect your life and the lives of humans more generally. Systemness is when people in the system become aware that they are part and parcel of a larger entity: their community, district, state, country, world, and universe. They become aware and conscious that there is a bigger system at work, that they should strive to understand it, influence it, and ultimately that they have a responsibility with others *to improve the system!*

I have already made the case that those at the top can never be good enough to run the show—war is too important to be left to the generals. Therefore, we have to build up the capacity of those at the local and middle levels to become better within their levels and across levels—to become system players.

In a practical sense if you are a leader the advice is *liberate* and interact with those below you (in the hierarchy) around a purposeful spirit work agenda. If you are on the receiving end in the hierarchy, don't define your role as doing what you are told (or for that matter always ignoring what you are told to do). Your role is not to literally obey the government agenda. Rather, it is to be a proactive consumer of policies in terms of local needs. If you examine all the vignettes in this book—all representing successful examples of improving the situations at stake—you see leaders who interact with the system up, down, and sideways. They certainly don't strike you as leaders doing what they are told.

In summary, I would say that if you build the agenda around spirit work; if you immerse yourself in contextual literacy; and if you are a system player (up, down, and sideways), you will do well by way of the system and vice versa. If there are enough of you doing this, you will have a good chance of changing the system for the better. The idea is to be successful in your own setting, as well as learning from and influencing aspects of the bigger system for the better. In short, systemness is a deliberate attempt to understand the system you are in, and the system you should want—and, of course, to help others lead in the same vein.

Greater clarity of action, which we will discuss in this chapter, is contained in Figure 5.1.

Action on system change occurs anytime school leaders step beyond the boundaries of their school to help change the environment in any significant way—to help change the community, for example. The concept *community schools* (CS)

Figure 5.1 The Elusiveness of System Change

The Elusiveness of System Change

- Don't define it from the top down.
- Define it from the bottom and middle up around deep learning.
- Systemness is when students, teachers, and others at the local and middle levels are helped to think differently about their systems leading to pathways of action that foster greater clarity, collaboration, and ownership of improvement.
- Increase people's consciousness that there IS a system.

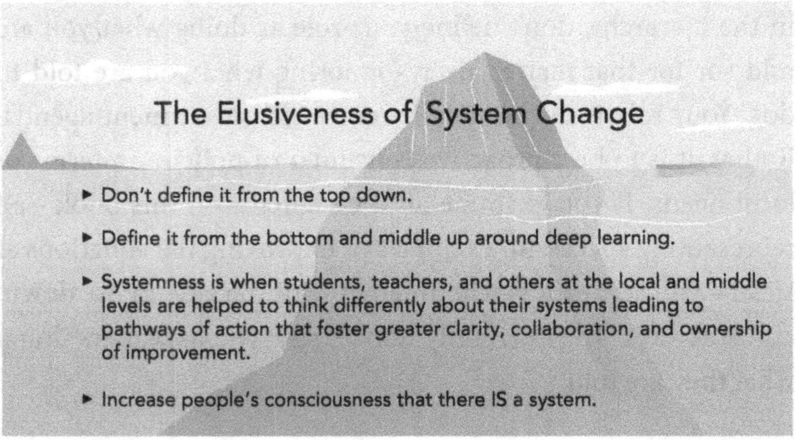

takes on a whole new meaning in 2022. CS as a concept and theory of action has been around at least since John Dewey. The movement has had its ups and downs trying to bring together the school as both a learning center and a community center. While there have been very powerful individual examples over the past 100 years, the movement never stuck or spread on any scale. Recently in California a new conceptualization has come on the scene—one that represents a move toward greater systemness. It is no longer a matter of getting the community involved but rather creating a new ecosystem where reducing poverty and increasing learning become embedded in the same strategy of changing the system. Our team is involved in the early stages of this movement where the state has allocated $4.1 billion to support these new developments. We are involved in several districts and counties, including San Diego County with its 42 districts and 500,000 students. It is too early to tell where the CS initiative is going but it is obvious that it is intended to be a significant *system change* with the principal front and center. At this early stage, I only want to point out CS as an example of a shift in the role of the principal that takes them into new system territory. System change means that one is both more grounded locally and more plugged in to regional and state developments.

Let's return to Ben Adlard primary school in northern England from Chapter 3—a great example of spirit work. We interviewed Marie-Claire Bretherton, the principal, in 2018. Recently, I began to wonder about the school in two new respects: What happened to it in the pandemic; and, related, did they engage in community development and, if so, where did it lead? I am making two points here. One is that since CS was not on my radar in 2018, perhaps I missed some key aspects of this relationship. Second, in any case, 2022 represents a whole new ballgame. My claim in this book is that we have just entered an era where system transformation is about to become (if it hasn't already) the centerpiece of improving learning and well-being. And of course, this means the principal is front and center in this third area—systemness for maximizing change. I figured that the current circumstances, and the leadership therein, would have made Benji ahead of its time in partnering with the community, so I doubled back to check. The following vignette is long, but I believe it nicely captures the depth of challenge and richness—and even clarity—of the solution as the principal (Marie-Claire Bretherton) and her chief assistant (Sam Coy) team up to work with the whole regional system.

Ben Adlard Revisited

It might be helpful to start with the official definition of California's new conception of community schools as expressed by one of the districts we work with—Vista Unified Community School District (VUSD) in San Diego County:

> A family-centered, equity-driven hub that serves every child and strengthens our community through partnerships that provide comprehensive wraparound services in health, wellness, and education.
>
> Community School Charge: To see and embrace each student with a comprehensive community support system of integrated services that are equity-driven, inclusive, and impactful. (2022)

In due course (beyond this book) I will report on VUSD's progress in relation to this aspiration, but let's consider what Benji did (we could add, without any official policy guiding them). I present the Benji vignette in two parts: one referring to the pandemic; the other focusing on parent and community relationships. There is some detail here, but the case warrants it. Successful cases always have good detail: specificity without imposition!

Principal Vignette 5.1a: Marie-Claire Bretherton, Ben Adlard Primary School, England; Pandemic Time

In Principal Bretherton's own words: When we were told that schools should close during the pandemic, we were obviously very concerned for the Benjamin Adlard community, pupils, and families. From the offset it was clear the school would have to step up to ensure the well-being and safety of the families we serve, within a community that was already vulnerable. The area the school serves is ranked as the 24th most deprived out of 32,844 neighborhoods in England. The challenges our community already faced had the potential to profoundly impact on pupils: high levels of deprivation; social issues within and sometimes between families; significant levels of unemployment; small, cramped housing conditions; little or no technology or broadband; no green spaces/parks in the local area; limited wider social or care services in the proximity. It was evident the community would be hit

(*Continued*)

hard, and with very few places to turn. The school is the community connector, and a mutually trusted lynchpin. We knew that the community would look to us, to the leaders they trusted to help them.

As always, the staff were fully aligned with our vision to make a difference, and we did exactly this. Initially communicating the message that the teachers, leaders, and support staff were still there for them, and that the school was still open and able to help, was vital. We needed to remain visible, at the point when families began to feel most isolated, and it looked like everything was closing up. (As an aside, the way Benji's pupils feel about the school cannot be underestimated. The last day of every term is often tinged with sadness and loss for some pupils. They would far rather be in school every day than at home, as for some, the relationship they have with the school staff is their only secure attachment. Lockdown for them could have been like a bereavement.)

We as leaders routinely walked the streets, offering reassurance to pupils and parents, answering questions about what they were allowed to do and not allowed to do, and keeping close to families. Throughout the period of lockdown, the new head of school (Luke Lovelidge) and executive headteacher (Sam Coy) were always on-site—providing reassurance to all, and in particular to the staff team who were going over and above what was asked of them.

Over the lockdown our work focused on the following:

- The school continued to have high numbers of pupils attend school, selecting all vulnerable and SEND [special education] pupils to attend every day, so we could care for them and educate them in school in carefully managed environments. Ensuring our staff felt safe and confident in maintaining a warm and nurturing environment despite the use of masks, and social distancing, was a challenge but one we overcame. We maintained daily contact with our most vulnerable families.
- Having established regular contact with all families by phone, at least twice a week, (and by dropping by and knocking on doors during community walk arounds) we quickly knew when some families were beginning to struggle. We offered respite care, to give parents and children a break from one another and a change of environment. This was above and beyond what the government could mandate. And for some pupils and families a lifesaver, as home life in lockdown became fraught. We set up rotations on a weekly basis, and through this maintained contact with every pupil and family.
- We very quickly used our community links to source laptops for pupils, through donations from businesses and contacts established in the wider town, and long before the government provided tech, we had already got 100 families set up to access learning online.

(*Continued*)

- We further developed our social media strategy (Twitter) to build a sense of connectedness, sharing lockdown journeys, encouraging and celebrating achievements at home, and keeping the school family connected—very much with a "we are in this together" mantra.
- We asked every member of the staff to film themselves reading a chapter of a book, and released a new chapter every day, to keep relationships strong. Although there was lots of online content being created by the government and others, we needed to retain our own personal connections and content. We used YouTube as a platform that could be accessed on mobile phones, making it more accessible. Many lessons were filmed by staff, just using their own phones, to share with families—including phonics lessons for our pre-readers and younger pupils.
- Even with the tech we have provided, we still had many families with no internet and with lots of families with multiple children to support at home. So we set up "work pack" collection points—to provide parents with an opportunity to safely visit the school to collect learning packs (and return completed work for marking). This was also strategic, as we could engage in conversation and assess the mental well-being of our parents, without intrusion. When parents couldn't collect, we would drop off at their front door to do the same. The use of physical work packs also had an educational benefit, as we knew that pupils would still be using fine motor

skills, using pencils, etc. A skill that we knew would go underdeveloped if we just used online resources.

- Stationary pick up points were provided, for art and crafts as well as basic resources.
- Reading book stations were also set up for parents and pupils to collect new books, these included books for parents.
- We were also mindful of the limitations of the local area, so we offered families slots in the forest school (the only green space in the area) to exercise, get fresh air, and have space to run and climb. We also set weekly exercise and well-being challenges for families and pupils to do together.
- The wider issues our community faced included basic needs, so we continued to offer support with accessing wider services, making phone calls, filling out forms, ringing landlords and the council, etc. We opened our own "food banks" and controlled collection slots in an area outdoors so families could come and collect a weekly supply of food.
- The family support worker and SENCO [special education] were relentless in their communication and support for individual families—working closely with social services to bridge the Covid gap.
- The school even went as far as to offer haircuts to the boys, when parents didn't have the resources or skills to do this themselves—providing dignity and creating yet another opportunity for contact and support.

(*Continued*)

The impact of the school's work during the pandemic meant the school kept its community identity, trust wasn't dampened, and, in fact, bonds were strengthened. Finally, when the country came out of the height of the pandemic, the community recognized the school cared—and that it was true to its mission—"we make a difference." This relational approach meant pupils returned excited, connected, and the hangover from the pandemic was not seen in the way other schools reported.

However, lockdowns clearly did have a negative impact for pupils overall. Speech and language acquisition and skills for all pupils but particularly younger pupils starting the school has been at an all-time low. Pupils academic progress suffered despite a strong remote program as pupils didn't get the richness of everyday school life—feedback, instruction, questioning, challenge, correction, etc. Additional socio-economic factors have meant that poverty is now at a record high, with 80% of pupils receiving pupil premium grants (free school meals).

But as always at Benjamin Adlard, due to the focused mission and the clarity of what needs to be done for the local community, the school will excel and continue to turn weaknesses and challenges into its strengths, do what needs to be done, and do what it does best—leave a legacy of love. (interview, July 2022).

Wow! Schools that had their act together prior to the pandemic fared better, and indeed figured out how to increase their effort. Work that appears hopeless exhausts people; when there is trust, strong teams, and cohesive relationships, hard work can be energizing (there are limits to be sure; strong groups monitor and attend to their own well-being). What I thought might be additionally revealing—what Marie-Claire and Sam learned about their approach to and experience with parents and community—the topic I had missed in 2018, but now (2022) take up in detail. The vignette is rather extensive because the situation warrants such a portrayal. Moreover, school and community development *together* represents a new mark of *systemness*.

Principal Vignette 5.1b: Marie-Claire Bretherton, Sam Coy, Ben Adlard Primary School, England.

Marie-Claire (MC):

There is some nod toward parents and the community in the inspection framework, but it doesn't really say to what extent and for what purpose. When we arrived, the school was very much isolated from its community. Parents and the kind of wider community services, if you like, were well at arm's length. And I think the feeling from staff was, what's the point of really doing a parents' evening, for example, because they didn't come; they didn't turn up. And you know, what's the point of really expecting our parents to engage in anything around home learning because lots of them can't read, lots of them can't contribute anyway. What's the point of having parents in the school to volunteer or help with stuff because they're more hassle than they're

(*Continued*)

worth? And actually, they didn't want to? And there was a bit of a sort of sense of kind of "them and us" with the community. I would also say that the way that schools are funded, there isn't any funding to pay for the luxurious roles, like having family support workers or community support workers. And so you're kind of having to grapple within your own budget to find resources to put leaders into those sorts of roles. There is funding available externally and we have bid for grants and bits and pieces as time's gone on. But a) that takes a specific skill set, and b) the time that it takes to kind of bring that stuff in, and it's always short-term funding rather than long-term.

I would also say that some of our teachers would say, "We know how to teach but we've never really been taught how to engage with parents or how to work with wider communities." That's a skill set; it's not necessarily developed, even as leaders really. So, I guess on arrival, there was just a real sense of we did need to do something to engage parents in the wider community, but actually it needed to start with the staff and the vision, and it was related to capacity-building. It meant challenging the mindset of the staff colleagues, in that there was just lots of assumptions and lots of judgment and lots of "them and us" and lots of "othering," if you like, between the staff team and the wider kind of community, as if the community was something to be able to defend against rather than to participate in.

Sam:

Yeah, I think the school was seen as a weak school in the area as well. The numbers were low. The narrative locally and in the area. around the school and community didn't necessarily help that either. And it didn't help the staff to feel that kind of sense of pride within the school because it was seen as, you know, the school that no one is sent to.

MC:

I remember the first big battle and actually some I think saw it just like that. I said, "Okay, we're going to run the parents' evening and we're going to try and get parents to come into school and actually, like have conversations with the staff." The staff were right: attendance was shocking. So few parents would cross the threshold into the building or even, to be frank, come into the playground. And we did a big sort of exercise around well, what are all the barriers that would mean that parents would find that difficult, you know, intimidation about being in a school, the fact that parents evening is after school when it's tea-time and the kids need feeding? The fact that a lot of parents have got multiple kids. So who looks after the other ones? A lot of them are single parents so they haven't got a support network over a period of time. Just breaking down some of those barriers was essential, for example putting on like a family meal where they could bring their granny if they

(*Continued*)

wanted, bring the older kids, bring the babies. We put on free food, free childcare, like let's find a way of bringing a bit of buzz to the room and just raising expectations of staff around giving the teachers targets around building relationships with parents, and then building that personal interaction of going and finding them at the gate or ringing them at home or encouraging them to have a conversation. It was very much around starting small, giving the staff some hope that actually they could have a meaningful conversation with parents, giving parents a good experience of the school and of staff and helping them to feel proud of their kids and all of the that very basic trust relationship-building stuff.

Sam:

We continued along these lines, and I think we did three more parents' evenings where we had had the meal and then obviously once parents had bought into that and kind of trust was built. And now the school consistently gets 90%-plus attendance every parent's evening. So there's kind of that huge movement. I'd say by the following October there was consistently mid 80s of percent of attendance. But on top of that we called all the parents that didn't attend and ask them what the barriers were for not attending and just had a conversation with them anyway. You couldn't really avoid it because you just got a phone call anyway. So you might as well have come and you get left alone. Over time, parents engage and once that engagement comes they want to come because they like being in school and they like being in the buildings.

MC:

And I think as well just being able to find lots of ways of celebrating their children. So you know, the sort of traditional academic, we're going to tell you how far behind they are in reading, writing, and math, not exactly the nicest thing for a parent to hear. But getting our staff to talk about the child in the broadest sense talk about their kindness, their teamwork, what they're like at play times. Talk about their talents, their friendships, and broaden the dialogue about the child. We wanted parents to go away feeling good about their kid because we knew that would strengthen relationships at home as well. And that in and of itself, building that dialogue and that secure relationship between parent and child would have ongoing positive impact. So that I think that parents' evening thing was kind of stage one and then alongside that we needed to tackle the kind of home learning barrier and knowing our community. It wasn't ever really going to work to send home lots of academic type of homework because the children, the kids are going to struggle, you know, until they've got certain levels of independence, but also the parents themselves, the intimidation that I know many of them have

(*Continued*)

around not being able to do basic math or not being able to read or write fluently themselves. So we went down a route of setting up like project-based home learning with fairly broad activities, and actually in many cases, multiple choice of here are a number of different things you could choose to do at home and things that those parents could do with their child that were art things or craft things or take a photograph or, you know, draw a map of some things to things that were fairly low, low key really, but that could build like a positive contribution so parents could feel like they could do something with their child at home to support their learning and feel like they're participating in whatever the topic was. We were just using social media to really celebrate what these kids brought in, regardless of what sort of state it was in. Just celebrating engagement basically and saying, look, this parent has helped their child to do something at home that they can bring in and be proud of and celebrate. Some parents began just feeling really proud of the fact that the school was saying what you're doing is enough, what you're contributing to with your child is having an impact.

Sam:

We made sure we shared every single aspect of positivity around engagement as a strategic kind of approach. It was communicated to staff, if someone brings something in that's on the back of an envelope that has been sent through the post, then you know, celebrate it, and then understand that they probably haven't got any paper and pens at home. So next time, give out paper and pens. It was kind of a mass celebration, the work and all the kids used to send all the home-learning projects used to come to the office were kind of like a sticker and a chat and a picture and, you know, that was that was a really massive part around kind of absolutely celebrating any aspect of engagement. And then we set up lunchtime home-learning clubs for the kids that we knew would struggle to do it at home, which sounds a bit weird because they were doing it in school. But we knew that there were some kids that would get some real positivity around that but didn't necessarily have the family structure or even just the quiet place to be able to do the work. So, they would come in at lunchtime, and we had an after-school Home Learning Club. Kids actually just wanted to come. Kids were going home and saying I've been to the office for positive things. We were all really positive around kind of building that trust and that feeling of community within the school.

MC:

Well, I think basically that whole piece of work around trust and engagement was very much about a wider goal actually which was about kind of the wraparound services and care that we knew we could broker and support families with. So I would say that

(*Continued*)

what we tried to do is become basically a mutually trusted linchpin between families and services for those who would otherwise be fairly isolated and transient. And social care, police community support mental health support, housing all became integrated.

We were building that level of trust with families where you can be really honest with them and you can call a spade a spade and you can say, actually, your care of your child's not quite up to scratch and we know you're struggling with housing or you're struggling with debt or you're in a domestic abuse relationship or wherever it might be having those trusting relationships with parents to be able to say we can help. We've got people who we actually ended up being employed in the school who could meet some of those wider social needs and be that kind of connecting point for families. The fact that their child is still in nappies and still has a dummy in their mouth and can't annunciate any sounds and parents just sort of accepting that: "well, that's just the way they are" rather than thinking there are some wider social needs here. Being able to have the trust with parents to be able to say, come on, we're going to help you get a speech therapist to have a look at, you know, whatever it might be, that if parents didn't trust us and didn't think we valued their contribution in terms of parents evening and home learning, we wouldn't have had permission or the relationship to be able to have those conversations. What it led to was helping parents with wider social infrastructure around helping them with housing issues, helping with food-related issues, and actually just being able to be genuinely a hub for that community.

Sam:

I think that in turn, as well, academic performance improved, because just even the engagement level of kids, the fact that they were proud of being part of the school and part of the community meant they put more effort in the classroom. So we had a journey of, you know, we're going to aim to be the best school in Gainsborough and every assembly would talk to the kids about being the best school in Gainsborough. And then, you know, when things improve, we talked about being the best school in England and then when things improved after that, we talked about being the best school in the UK and then eventually it was the best school in the world, and it used to it became the things kids said in assembly—the kids saying "what we're aiming to be the best school in the world."

We knew there was the distrust of the police and health services and benefits and families and Jobs Center. So we had to start with building the trust of the parents to be able to then unlock that. Because once they trusted us, trusted the school and the vision, it was easy then to pinpoint and direct them to other

(*Continued*)

people that could help but it had to come through us. We had to be the centralized point. We couldn't just send them off to those people. We have to bring those people into school and use school as kind of community hub. So that's what we did. We have a bank for uniforms, food bank, adult learning project, training for adults around parenting, housing support. Pam, the lady in the office, even used to book an hour slot to do form fill in for anyone that needed their benefit claims or anything that they couldn't work out. She'd sit with them and just fill out forms. We also got some funding to run an adult learning project. Originally, we were hoping to get four or five. We put out like a leaflet in the Job Center. Basically, it was one day a week for a 10-week program parents that were unemployed, or anyone actually, we said anyone in the community from 18 to whatever their age was could come and they would come and take part in a 10-week program. And at the end of the program, they'd get like a generic reference just kind of talking about their attendance and the skills and stuff that they've done. And then we did like a CV writing workshop to try and help them into employment. So, we were hoping for five people we got 29 people attend and 27 of them attended all 10 sessions. We had people from the age of 18 to 65. So it was it was really positive and they didn't necessarily have to have a link to the school. It increased community presence.

MC:

Yeah, the staff, the staff were brilliant. I think the breakdown of judgmentalism was really quite significant. So instead of viewing the community and the parent community in a sort of deficit model in some kind of meritocracy-type thing, the staff actually really began to connect with the parents, like a vision for what flourishing looks like for our community and therefore understanding and seeing that supporting with some of those wider things actually would help them fulfill their ultimate vision. You know, Benji is not an easy place to work in in lots of ways. You get your heart broken year after year of stories of kids who don't have what's required and have horrible things happen to them, but the fact that the staff there take that responsibility so seriously, and they see that actually, that wider work is a way of us contributing to some of the social issues. So, you know, being able to identify safeguarding concerns much earlier, for example, is hugely powerful in terms of stopping stuff happening that could happen. I think the staff changed and grew. But we also made some really key appointments in the team and did a bit of reshuffling around roles and responsibilities. So, for example, somebody within the team did become a full-time family support worker and that was her entire job was around supporting families. And that was in addition to a full

(*Continued*)

time special needs leader who was able to work at sort of preschool age. So, teachers could focus on teaching but they could also participate in the wider kind of ambition for that community. I think that there is a parallel between our community relations and the school doing better—such as getting through the Ofsted inspection, and the award and various other things, staff's pride in the school and being proud for the right reasons. It was not just pride of academic achievement like kids who can read and write; of course, that's important. But they're also just proud of the fact that these kids have got better life chances going forward as a result of some of the really basic things that are within the curriculum like you know. Sam I'll never forget you like doing a boys club and teaching the Year 6 boys how to shave and how to tie a tie and how to do just some basic sort of fathering skills, parenting skills that quite a lot of the community wouldn't be able to do. I think it's really powerful around the staff feeling like they're making a contribution to humans having a better life rather than just some accountability system.

The funny thing is that agencies started to ask us for help—the police or social services at the council or whoever. They will ring Sam or they'll ring the school to say, "Can you help us engage with this family?" "Can you help us solve this social problem?" "We've got a drug issue here. Can you help us have that conversation with this person." So actually, it's trust coming the other way from some of those arm's-length services to actually see the school as having the potential as Sam said, to be that linchpin and that hub—a kind of parish for that community.

There's loads of challenges around. You know, the accountability systems and the inspection systems. They don't shout about community connection being an important part of the work. They don't necessarily value it to the same extent. But I would say, and Sam I don't know what you think of this, but the last inspection we had at Benji's the inspector did get it, it's just that the framework doesn't allow him to tick any boxes or write anything about it, but he absolutely got it at an emotional level, that this was far more than just educating some children. It was about transforming a community. I know that you [Fullan] talk about the levers and drivers for system change and all of that spirit work stuff that I've just loved to see, acknowledged, and recognized; and that could really unleash I think a lot of, you know, systemic change in community.

Sam:

I think on a really basic level as well, like we, we often focus on like the weaknesses when we go into an area so we'll look and we'll go, there's high mobility, transient population or you know, there's, you know, huge deprivation impairments in care and what we

(*Continued*)

do is we focus on the weakness and we talk about the weakness too much, it becomes just like a problem. Now, because it's already a problem, it becomes kind of embedded absolutely kind of in-depth problem. And one of the things we try to reverse is always looking at the problem and turn it into a strength. If you've got high transient population, you have to turn that into a strength. So your induction program for kids coming in and out to school has to be absolutely the best going. If you've got high deprivation, you've got to do everything that you can to counteract that deprivation. There's no point just keep going on about the deprivation being a problem. You've got to challenge the problem. You take something that is your weakness and you turn it into your strength. We would have loads of people coming to the school that would talk about high mobility among students and families, and ask us what we did about it. We would then share our induction program. I know that's a really simplistic way of looking at it, but you just turn a weakness into strength, and you power through with that and then everything else is consistent.

MC:

When you are fixing things you have to do the foundational stuff first—all around behavior and culture. There's no point giving my teachers a hard time about improving their teaching practice if they didn't have strong relationships with the pupils and if the pupils weren't actually able to listen to sit whatever it needed to be. And this is where the *Nuance* book resonated with me just so much was actually there's like an instinct you get like; it's almost like in the cells of your body you kind of just know instinctively that there is some doors that are meant to be pushed and opened and there are some quick wins and some early things you've got to do. It's almost like, I knew that we would be able to improve teaching, but I knew that we had to kind of get the right people in place first. So appointing Sam was absolutely top of my list. I need somebody in there full time every day, who's brilliant on behavior, who's brilliant on relationships. And once we've got that in place, then we can start to begin to look at some of those wider things. And actually by the end of it, when we had the final Inspection where they graded us as 'good', both the inspector and the other people in the team were so emotional about the journey the school had been on, they could genuinely tangibly see that transformation. We did do the family community stuff we did get academic success and the inspector could see that for sure.

We need people who are prepared to do a journey of being a human being alongside the parents and the

(*Continued*)

community and understanding that the vast majority of those parents love their kids and they want their kids to do well. They might not know how, they might not have the skills, they might not have had good experiences, but genuinely, most of those parents want to get it right. And if you can, if you can sort of accept that and understand that you're a human as well. There is just a really powerful leveler in terms of that relationship of trust that we've described.

Sam:

You can teach someone to teach, you can't teach someone to have authentic relationships with kids. Anyone coming to look for a job, it was all over the job adverts, it was all we talked about the presentations was set around the vision, you know, everything that they were going to deliver was they knew that if they were coming for a job you had to be engaged in the school journey and approach. Marie-Claire was welcoming on the gate, and any opportunity would walk the streets. We'd walk around, you pop into the corner shop, and you'd go and knock on a door to get a kid to come to school in the morning. But you'd pop in. You'd knock on a few doors and say hello, as you're walking down, you become a community figure, which the community looks at as somebody that they would trust. But, you know, it's not the safest of areas if I'm honest, but I have never felt in the last five years that I was unsafe walking around the area because I knew everyone. People would say hello, people would wave. If there was problem after school, rather than picking up the phone I'd drive to the house, and call in and have cups of tea out of mugs that you probably never wanted to drink out of, but you did it because it was part of that engagement. You know, we've done things like fitted washing machines for families, I've crawled underneath pipes, at 10 past five on a Friday night and tried to fit a washing machine just to build that level of trust for a new family that might have joined the community. I think it is all around that having a vision but building trust on every level. And you can only do that by really engaging in the community. And I think sometimes leaders probably get that wrong by trying to be aspirational instead of being relational for starters. But actually sometimes by getting in at their level, joking and laughing on the gate and, you know, having all these kinds of conversations, probably some people would frown upon and say, that's not a professional conversation to be having but actually all of that builds trust. And once you've had

(*Continued*)

those conversations and parents in those areas feel that they can talk to you on that level you can then have the more difficult conversations that Marie-Claire talks about in terms of talking about child-care, talking about these things because they know that you're invested in doing it for their kids, and that you're not trying to tell them what to be trying to help them. And I think that's probably the skill set. It's about trying to convince the community that you're there to help not tell them what to do, because a lot of them will have spent years being told what to do with no answers. That is what it is, is you know, being part of them. You can't be the community school, but not be part of the community. I mean, don't get me wrong. I didn't go to the level of buying the house across the road from school. But you know, if I'd have had to have done that I would have. And that's the point. You have to be really, really part of the community.

MC:

The school received the prestigious Making a Difference award. This is about saying to our parents, you know what you can make a difference in the smallest way for your child, by helping them. You can make a difference in your community by the person that you are and the relationships that you have. So, it's kind of yes, of course, the academic stuff is important. But we don't want any

> ceiling to be put there. We also want to recognize that being part of a community is about showing up as a person and a human being and making a contribution to those around you. You meet the community where they are and you tell them stories about where that community can go. But you recognize that there's so many different ways people can make a difference and that it's actually about participation and character and hope within those relationships.

Brilliant observation by Sam: "Leaders have to be relational before they can be aspirational". I believe that Ben Adlard is a precursor to new versions of co-development between communities and schools. In some ways this will be increasingly complex because the problems are deeper and more multifaceted. In other ways, it might be helped by new conceptions of well-being and learning, new capacities of community agencies, more powerful and usable technology, and the greater role of students as changemakers (see Fullan, 2022; Fullan & Quinn, forthcoming). Students and parents in such situations have tremendous potential to become good at learning and good at life. A new brand of community schools linked to learning and well-being strategies, funded by the state, and led by strong school and community leaders could make a world of difference.

In the meantime, let's see what a more favorable set of conditions can produce from scratch.

A More Privileged Start-Up

Bill Hogarth Secondary School (BHSS) in York Region just north of Toronto opened its doors in November 2017 with its first group of Grade 9 and 10 students. The school was named after a long-standing director (superintendent) of the district. Its inaugural principal, selected from within the district, was Janani Pathy, who just finished her term at BHSS in June 2022. By that time there was a full cohort of 1600 students across Grades 9–12.

Without any system direction, Pathy decided to focus on the 6Cs; in fact, each of six external pillars of the school spell out vertically one of the 6Cs. I have had some relationship with the school since its opening, but its development has been wholly driven by Pathy, and the staff, students, and parents of the community. The school catchment consists of large numbers of new homes built during the last eight years. It is a highly diverse community that would be considered middle class. I selected this case because there is an explicit commitment to develop students who can cope with and influence the world for the better—hence its connection to systemness.

Jeff Ikler, as part of his *Getting Unstuck* series, interviewed Pathy in 2021 about her role as founding principal. The vignette here is based on this interview.

Principal Vignette 5.2: Janani Pathy, Bill Hogarth Secondary School (BHSS) (adapted from Ikler, 2021b)

Pathy:

We really believe in each student's potential to be a leader. In fact, that is our focus, student leadership. So right from Grade 9, we encourage our students to enroll in our leadership course in Grades 9 or 10. And then again, a leadership course of their choice in Grade 11 or 12. Because we don't define leadership as the person that's outgoing and is just vocal we see leadership as the ability of someone to have a positive influence on others. Everyone has leadership potential. And if every student we can develop their confidence if they too, can make a change, they too can have an impact.

I've had the pleasure of opening a new school in York region in Ontario and we opened the school in 2017. The school is located in a place called Markham, which happens to be diverse in terms of its cultural makeup. The families are first or second generation Canadian and tends to be a middle class, SES demographic. The unique part of our school is that it has a very focused vision and approach to teaching and learning.

The students that began in the school helped to co-create that culture—from selection of school colors,

(*Continued*)

a school mascot, a school motto, to the actual vision of the school. It came together from input from staff, students, and parents, and I think that is one of the reasons why everyone can speak so strongly to it. The vision is grounded in the deep pedagogies for learning. Our focus is on what we fondly call our 6Cs. Everyone sees value in that, beyond learning science, math, history, and geography. We all know that content is important, but families, students, and staff, everyone sees the value of those skills in terms of this school.

You would see the 6Cs in many ways. When you walk through classrooms, you would see for example, the commitment to collaboration in the way in which the classroom is set up—the way in which the furniture has been intentionally selected, and the way in which students are grouped. If we believe in collaboration, we have to provide the actual structures and classrooms. You would see the commitment to the 6Cs in the actual work that's happening. Students will start in Grade 9 asking students about an idea, a question that they wish to explore in the idea of a passion project. And we know that just open-ended inquiry does not work well. Of course, it has to be structured in such a way that allows students to look and to think and to explore their interests, and then to narrow in on an area that's aligned with that particular content or skills that the English courses is supposed to teach.

But what we find when you look at the products that come out of these genius hour projects is such depth in terms of thinking, in terms of students being able to collaborate with each other as well as their incredible ability to communicate.

Staff approaches teaching content from an equity framework. We critically analyze, we interrogate what you know, systemic pieces, we might inadvertently be perpetuating and what we might do differently. For example, whose history are we teaching? Whose voices are missing in that history? When we look at the kids in our classroom, can they identify with the content being taught, or are we valuing what their families have brought to Canada? Our history department approached me to ask if they could deviate from doing a traditional final written exam, to doing one where there would be discussion and debate about what it means to be Canadian and can we be proud of Canada's history? Keeping an open-ended approach to a culminating task, but that task draws on all the different units and cycles of learning that took place throughout so that students could demonstrate their knowledge, but do it in such a way that they could draw from the wide variety of learning experiences that they've had? That would be an example of assessment not being content driven, but one that is very much relevant. It also allows teachers to be responsive to

(*Continued*)

what is happening in the world around us, as we know right now. So many issues of social inequities and justice are surfacing. We feel we have a moral responsibility to engage students in this discussion, so that they can also move on and become agents of change.

Students are actively part of the school and the classroom community from the day that they walk in the Learning Community, the expectations of those learning is co-created with the students and you will see those on the walls in the classrooms or on the Google Classrooms. When it comes to the actual tasks, certainly there is ongoing opportunities for students to do their own self-reflection, as well as to provide peer feedback. There is guidance in terms of how to provide feedback. How do you start with providing something that is a strength? How am I to then lead into an area where you can let your peer know that this is an area of growth? Teaching students how to provide feedback is also important so that they will continue to feel to be allowed themselves to be vulnerable to receive that feedback in a way that is not threatening. That also encourages discussion, the idea of being that critical friend, without criticizing someone and making them feel small in a classroom. So how do we have that collegial, critical thinking happening in a classroom and that's very much about teaching, teaching how to do that.

Learning has to be something that is living and breathing continuum. When we say we have communication as a focus, what does that mean? At the beginning when we opened, we established a team, we call them our 6Cs, think tank of teachers from across departments. They met, and they created a continuum where they said okay, when students are in Grade 9, what should we be able to see in terms of their communication skills when they move to Grade 10. And by the time we shake their hand as they graduate in Grade 12, how should we have seen their communication skills develop so they co-created from their past experiences what they felt students should be able to do across subject areas. It's not specific to English or to science, but in fact, should be expected in math, in tech studies, in drama. It is more than the anchor charts on the walls and the banners in the Grand Hall. It is actually what is happening on a day-to-day basis in class.

Jeff Ikler asked: How do you teach them to be collaborative versus just throwing them in a group?

Again, it goes back to many factors: 1) as I mentioned before is structure in terms of the classroom, but 2) is also just intentional decisions around instruction. We do not have, for example, computer labs in the school. We have chosen to have carts of technology available. But even in those carts, a class may only access one cart that is 15 Chromebooks versus an entire set.

(*Continued*)

Because the idea is that students have to understand that when they're collaborating, they have to talk to each other as opposed to four people sitting around a computer screen. So facilitating just even access to resources in such a way that pushes collaboration is important. The second part is establishing what that looks like. We've seen incredible ways in which teachers nurture collaboration. At the entry level, in a junior course, a teacher might start by saying well, what's effective collaboration? What's really bothered you about, quote 'group work' in the past?

And then what do we want collaboration to look like? And then they'll ask that critical question, what is the difference between group work, teamwork, and collaboration. Is collaboration really building on the best ideas that the group has to offer? We put all of our ideas on the table? We assume positive presuppositions about all those ideas and then we take pride in the fact that it is not whose idea was, you know, brought forward at the end, but how might we all build upon that idea? As a group and take pride as a group? The students have responded in ways that I could not have imagined, and when I say that in the most positive ways, in ways that I feel like we truly underestimate our youth and their ability to think critically, their ability to be so empathetic, to listen to each other. We have had a very interesting course run in the past couple of years, which is a cross-curricular course between English and history. And when you talk about collaboration, where students are working on content in two courses together, you should see the way in which the projects are created by the students because it's led by an inquiry question, and then the depth to which they go because the conditions have been created for them to feel comfortable with each other, to challenge each other in a very supportive way. And to really see excellence emerge in so many different ways is how I would summarize it.

Parents have responded so positively. I was nervous when we opened. I thought parents would be more traditional in their approach. But I feel it works because the 6Cs just makes sense, right? Like who doesn't want their child to think critically, doesn't want their child to have excellent communication skills, who doesn't want their child to have solid character in a world where students are faced with so many ethical choices? [*Author note: I am aware that some parents do not want schools to delve into what they see as family matters, but in BHSS this is worked out with students and the community.*] So the 6Cs have been one way in which I feel like parents feel very comfortable sending their children to our school. Parents also recognize through our academic standing through our provincial scores on standardized tests, that teaching the 6Cs is not at the expense of academic excellence. In fact, it promotes academic excellence, and I think that has also been one way to affirm their confidence. In sending their children here.

Jeff asks about leadership courses that students take:

Well, because we really handpick teachers to be in that course, kids are going to have teachers that are

(*Continued*)

super enthusiastic and welcome them in, and even the child that may never have said anything in Grade 8 is going to find a way in which their voice is going to be heard. The structure of the class is certainly building community in those classes, but then looking at the mindsets and habits of effective leaders, as well as practicing those in relation to three components in terms of how might I lead in my class, how might I lead in the school, and then what might I do to lead in the community whether it's local or global? And so that's how they approach the course.

They also practice leading. The teachers are really terrific in the way they scaffold that. It might start in the first month about everyone in the class having to lead an icebreaker activity, and for some students that might be so natural, and for others, they might be like, oh my goodness, I can't believe I have to lead 30 students. So there's coaching that's happening on the side. And then there's also the way in which those teachers build enthusiasm so they will always ensure that every student has a positive reaction to the activity. There'll be different coaching pieces in terms of how do we give our teammates and our peers positive feedback. Okay, what is one thing that we can take away that we could share so that everyone's confidence is built? And then there are many, many opportunities that are available. Our leadership teachers have done a great job in terms of making a partnership with the seniors home across the street. So one of the leadership activities is to engage in having that intergenerational connection. We talk about Valentine's Day and how it's so commercial in terms of the type of quote love that is, you know, promoted through greeting cards and chocolates and roses. And what does that mean, right when it is unconditional? What does it mean when our grandparents and our parents and our family members give us love and why don't we celebrate that on Valentine's Day, so they go over on Valentine's Day, but to share a different type of love, is one example.

In hiring we look for teachers who have shown through their experience or through their interview that they are open to learning that they are very open in terms of their mindset and their approach. We look for teachers that have demonstrated that they do more than teach between nine and four, that they are able, and they have contributed to a school community in so many ways. Because when we are building a new school and new school culture, we need everyone to be part of what we call our BHSS family. It can't be a job it has to be a calling. For anyone who really believes in the true purpose of education, which is to really tap into the potential of every child and make sure that we help them achieve that. If we can see evidence of examples where people have been risk takers, are they open to it? They have demonstrated that they have taught in different ways, assessed in different ways. Or that they are open to it. Then as long as people are eager and willing and open minded, we are ready to have them on our team.

When you are growing and hiring so many people you have to understand the why. I foresee the challenge of a school like ours is the massive growth we have had, so we opened in 2017 at 450 students and in September

(*Continued*)

2021 we are almost going to be at 1,600 students. This past June alone, we hired 25 new teachers. When we have that kind of growth where I started with 30 staff and now I'm over 100. Maintaining that momentum and focus and feeling of community and culture is critical. What we have done over a short history is, each time a new group of teachers joins us for the next school year, we do an orientation in terms with potential new staff: This week sort of gave you a snippet of who we are. Here are our core commitments, our 6Cs, leadership, equity, and well-being. And we have a focus on student leadership. So these and this is what it looks like so people can see what it looks like. And that is not delivered by the administration, but that orientation is hosted by other teachers so that it is by teachers for teachers.

We also focus on well-being for all. For students we opened the school based on board data that also suggested mental health was an area that schools needed to focus on so we started with a weekly mindful practice, called it mindful Mondays, where every Monday when we start the morning announcements, we start with a mindful practice. It might be a deep breathing exercise where we say to students, if you're feeling anxious before a test or anything else, before a job interview, as you're riding the bus, you can just do this breathing exercise. We do it in terms of just being present exercises, to be present to be aware so you don't allow the circumstances to overwhelm you. Teachers might choose to do these mindfulness activities before a quiz or before a test or before presentation. We also explored physical wellness and what that might look like in terms of movement breaks. A wellness Google

Classroom was created by staff so that ideas could be shared. And there are tons of activities where any new teacher who's just looking for an idea to incorporate wellness in their classroom can go to an online classroom filled with resources, but it is something that we model with staff at staff meetings at PA days in terms of doing these exercises together. But when we talk about the pandemic, and what we've learned is how social isolation can really have an impact. The value of the human connection has always been important at a new school, but we feel that has really helped keep us connected. At the beginning of the pandemic, in March [2020], we as a staff decided that we were going to do small video clips every week that we would then send out to our community through the newsletter and through our Twitter account. And at first it was like we just missed you and were thinking about you. And then it was just on different themes that would emerge in a particular week. But the feedback from the community and from the students was so unexpected because this was a little bit of a risk. How many of us really liked to be on camera and you know, we're sort of very comfortable in our classrooms, when you've got your small group, but when, you know an entire community can see it, but it was the feedback reaffirmed the importance that kids needed to see their staff. They needed to see the teacher that might not be their subject teacher but the one they really enjoyed saying hello to in the hallway, their basketball coach, whoever and we found those videos really helpful in connection. Those are just small examples of ways in which we really tried the importance of that human connection.

(*Continued*)

Jeff closes the interview with the question: How would you define your leadership philosophy?

> I feel like my leadership philosophy is one that is service oriented. I feel like my job is to serve the staff at the school in ways that uplift them in ways that empower them. Because in turn, my hope is that they also uplift and inspire their students. My wish is that every student feels seen, feels heard, feels like they come to a place that truly cares about them, hears about them as an individual and what they bring with cares about them in terms of their areas of growth, so we develop them. And I wish for students to feel like when they leave the school, this has been the best four years of their schooling experience because people really cared about them. But this was a class that had started with us in Grade 9 and was graduating in Grade 12. Of what it means to be part of the BHSS community. The way the staff came together to organize an event outside that was just so filled with warmth, with energy, with enthusiasm and the feedback that we got from parents like if you watch parents as they drove by, and the tears that came out of their eyes. They couldn't believe that in a pandemic, a school would take that time to celebrate their child in a certain way. Because there were balloons all over the place. We had a red carpet. Kids came, they got a photo with getting a diploma. But it was the idea that we are going to celebrate your child no matter what, because these last four years have been special, and it might not be in a banquet hall. It might not be in this grand, grand way that we might have done. If we could pack 1,000 people unmasked in a place, but with the limitations placed, we still want

every child to know that they mattered. And they felt that so I feel like that's true success. When even at times like this, a school community can come together.

My message is believe in yourself and believe in others and know that each one of us, each one of us, has the power to impact change and not to be limited by structures or systems because we have seen it happen from the ground up in terms of change. The work that we've been doing has certainly been based on New Pedagogies for learning so certainly I feel like this concept of engage the world to change the world, and to help humanity, is it's just inspiring. I also feel like authors like Brené Brown when they talk about, when she talks about, dare to lead and talk talks about the importance of courage, of humility of bravery, and what that really means to show up every day and lean, has had an influence in terms of my own thinking. And then I look at informal leaders, so people in our lives that come every day and motivated us and inspire us and that could be family. It could be your neighbor. It can be people that we the world doesn't see as a leader, but people that inspire us to be better to bring really the best version of ourselves. Who are those people? You know, and how can we sort of emulate that.

An interesting spinoff developed naturally at BHSS when the election for student council president 2022–2023 occurred. There were three female student candidates. They decided together that they would each select a C as their defining platform. Here they are in the words of each of the three students:

(*Continued*)

Collaboration:

One 6C that I find super important for being a president is collaboration. Collaboration is key. Because in the end as president, it's your goal to make everybody work together. It's not your ideas that are being shared, but you're simply bringing the voices of everyone else to the table, which is why it's such an important skill for a leader. For me, I demonstrate collaboration through business clubs, as well as many other extracurriculars because I helped my peers work together to reach a common goal and an innovative solution.

Critical Thinking

Hi, BHSS family. I am a student in Grade 11. And I'm beyond honored for the opportunity to run for student council president for the 2022–2023 school year. The 6Cs are an important set of values that the Hornet [BHSS nickname] community takes the heart. They include collaboration, character, creativity, critical thinking, citizenship, and communication, although all of them are important, out of the 6Cs, I believe that critical thinking is the most vital. Critical thinking allows you to evaluate your decision making at any level and how these decisions ultimately impact results. One of the most important aspects of critical thinking is to decide what you're aiming to achieve and then make a decision. Based on the large range of possibilities, making critical thinking the most versatile, but mainly, I believe that critical thinking is the most vital due to the fact that it can be applied to all the other five Cs. If you can utilize critical thinking and effective manner, you can easily excel in all the other Cs for instance, when solving a collaboration or communication issue, you can apply critical thinking to assess your decision making and actions to help further benefit the situation. This past year with all extracurricular events going online, it was extremely hard planning initiatives from York region's President's Council and communities Youth Council while maintaining the same quality. Hence, our teams learned how to power critical thinking skills, how to promote our events, such as using techniques like bingo cards and creative incentives. Thank you for the invitation to come out here today to speak about my favorite 6C and hope all of you have a great wonderful rest of your day.

Citizenship

In my opinion, each 6C carries a unique value which creates and brings importance to the role of student council president. Out of the six if I were to choose one, I think citizenship would be a strong root skill. Citizenship is a skill that correlates with the other 6Cs. Bringing it much more value once one has developed their mindset to become an active citizen. They would take the initiative to collaborate and communicate more effectively, creatively and critically think, which would then enhance their character as a whole. One way I chose to be an active citizen was by founding the South Asian student association here at Bill Hogarth all in hope to provide students with a safe platform to learn more about South Asian heritage's.

(*Continued*)

But also give them different opportunities to enhance their citizenship skills through this club. Thank you.

The Keys Are Yours

There you have it over the past three chapters. The three keys with strong principal vignettes. Systemness is perhaps the most difficult to grasp, but each of the keys leads to the others. Use any one well and you will find yourself heading toward the other two. Its best to take each chapter separately and let it take you within the domain while inevitably whetting your appetite for the other two. In the final chapter I will put them together. This will take us beyond the existence of the three keys and cause me, and you, to consider and grapple with the question: Where do we go from here? I don't fully know. I have to say, if there is a journey into the unknown, this must be it. But also, there is no denying that the eight principals featured in this book realized that they were dealing with complexities, unknowns, and boundless threats. Our principals don't think of the keys as providing immediate answers but rather as opening the right doors. They think of their roles as *future making*. Remember: the keys in question are for discovering powerful pathways and transforming systems. They can be valuable for both short-term actions and mid- to long-term solutions. In either case, you will be better off if you master the use of the three keys in combination.

At BHSS, no C is more privileged than another, and as you have just heard from the three students, whatever one you might start with you are inevitably drawn to the others. I bet you are wondering what C won. That's not the right question: all Cs lead to Rome!

CHAPTER ONE

The Three Keys: Picking Up the Pieces

CHAPTER TWO

A Long Time Coming

CHAPTER THREE

Spirit Work: The First Key for Maximizing Impact

CHAPTER FOUR

Contextual Literacy: The Second Key for Maximizing Impact

CHAPTER FIVE

Systemness in Action: The Third Key for Maximizing Impact

CHAPTER SIX

Future Making

CHAPTER · SIX

Future Making

What should be the principal's role in the future—assuming the future starts now? Let's revisit Chapter 1 where I introduced my *Six Reasons to be Optimistic About Learning in 2022* (Fullan, 2022):

1. Escaping a bad system
2. Recognizing and working with our best allies (students, teachers, parents, principals)
3. Well-being and learning are joining forces
4. New more powerful forms of learning on the rise
5. Diverse leadership will grow and present new benefits
6. Systems will begin to change

Escaping a bad system

Whether you call it inflection, projection, or speculation, I think the majority of people would agree it is time to act. Sometimes we live in a system where most people don't like the system we have. Maybe that has been the case for a long time, but I think that there is more self-awareness today, especially among the young—3-year-olds and up—that something is particularly awry that will have dire consequences in our lifetimes. I would venture to say that the percentage of young people aware of this potentially catastrophic situation has never been higher.

Most people understandably don't know what to do about it. But they probably would agree that focusing on well-being linked to learning—new and better learning than we have ever had before—might be a good route to take.

Recognizing and working with our best allies

Helping to lead us out of a bad system may be one role that many principals would love to take up. Then, where do we find our best allies in this mammoth undertaking. Not from those at the top in charge of the system. Even if they are inclined, they are unlikely to know what to do. Those bearing the brunt of a bad system are more likely to at least have a sense of where to start. The fact that the education system historically has segmented people does not help us discover who we can best team up with—teaching as the "lonely profession" did not get us off to a good start. And principals rarely see how those in the same role behave when they are going about their daily fare. We don't even know who our best allies might be (although the pandemic has helped sort out some hunches with respect to the "mights" and the "might not be's"). We will see later how the future of the teaching profession depends a great deal on the new role of the principal as connector and mobilizer within and external to the school.

Well-being and learning are joining forces

During COVID-19, many of us suffered more than ever before in our lifetime. We got to know too much about death, loneliness, and seeming hopelessness. We got to know what stress and anxiety really were. If we were lucky, we got to experience what helpfulness and kindness from strangers was—surprising revelations occurred. Many of us grasped what well-being or its opposite felt like and meant.

New more powerful forms of learning on the rise

Most of us probably would not have noticed that large gains were made in knowing what learning is, and how it can be dramatically accelerated when pedagogy and technology combine. More knowledge became available in the last 20 years than in the previous forever ago (does it really matter here whether it was 130,000 years ago or 2.5 million?). Much of this new knowledge has become crystalized in the new neuroscience like SoLD (science of learning and development; Cantor & Osher, 2021), in our own NPDL (Quinn et al., 2020), and in our new *Drivers* book: well-being and learning; linking social intelligence with machine intelligence; equality investments; and greater systemness (Fullan & Quinn, forthcoming). The point is that it is that we have barely begun to draw on our new knowledge and related strategies, which by now are becoming quite powerful and known.

Diverse leadership will grow and present new benefits

The long-standing finding about success—that it boils down to leadership—is almost useless as a starter. Success occurs only in a small minority of possible cases, so it is hard to generalize. If it is only in a tiny minority, how can we possibly count on it? But there are new hints: the population is diverse; leadership can come from many directions; success can be more likely if we cultivate heterogenous leadership that can work in teams. Diverse, coordinated leadership is the way of the future—young and old, various ethnicities, and gender differences. And most of all, leadership upward (from the bottom and middle) is growing.

Systems will begin to change

No kidding, Sherlock! More helpfully, can we combine the previous five forces to figure out how systems can change and what new, better systems can replace them? This brings us back to leadership and to the question: Can an overhauled conception of the principal's role become one of those evolutionary phenomena that seems to pop up just in time? Think of evolution as the product of the interactive combination of genetics, culture, and consciousness (Campero, 2019). In such a scenario, principals are in a position to be a catalytic force for system change.

Finally, treat the six reasons as an opportunity. Consider the plight of the historical principalship: "What do you want me to do, anyway?" Realize that we have an evolutionary crisis/opportunity on our hands. This might be the very time to generate, be clear about, and cultivate the role of the principal that we should want and do need for this decade and more. Principals especially should seize the moment.

The Journey to a New World

In this book I have confined myself to the Western world, and I do not claim to generalize beyond that. However, we do work in the Global South (e.g., Latin America). I can say that there is an increasing interest in school leadership as part and parcel of system reform and that these countries have some advantages over Western countries: for example, reform-minded youth; starting with advanced technology; entering with a sense of urgency; and community mobilization. Look for future work from us, especially from our team member Santiago Rincón-Gallardo and his work on leadership for liberating learning.

In the meantime, we should conclude with our own history and where we are today. I cannot take the space to cover in detail the last 200 years of the role of the school leader. But we can do enough to arrive at a good sense of the evolution of the principalship in the context of what might be the most powerful new direction—one that is clear enough, desirable enough, and urgent enough to proactively cultivate in practice—including an invitation to incumbents in the role to help make it happen. From logs to bricks, the one-room schoolhouse with a teaching principal and a handful of teachers truly was one-stop shopping. For a long time, principals "managed" a small local community addressing basic education and small-scale community needs. The modern school was created in the United States during the last half of the nineteenth century into the twentieth, establishing a system of professional teachers, a teaching principal, and basic curriculum content. The principal was clearly the local education leader for a given community with definable boundaries.

During this period, the principal was assessed on being a good manager. If the school ran smoothly—little conflict, reliable teaching staff, balanced budget—all was good. Society became more serious about schools in the 1960s—some say arising from the Russians beating the United States to space with Sputnik in 1957. In the following paragraphs I use the United States as the marker because the data are more available, and its education history is similar to most Western countries, although when it comes to actual cases and related strategies, local context is always key. Change must be customized to the local setting.

Until the end of the twentieth century, the education system operated as a loosely coupled system. Warning shots were fired in 1983 with the publication of a US National Commission on Excellence in Education: *A Nation at Risk: The Imperative for Education Reform*—an urgent call to action without any specifics about how to get there. For the rest of the century school systems could act, but most didn't know what to do as tension mounted. A bipartisan intended solution in the form of *No Child Left Behind* (NCLB) was legislated into action, signed by George W. Bush in January 2001. The act required "standards and related tests" be established that required all students across the grades to be assessed in reading and math according to adequate yearly progress (AYP). If AYP was not achieved, various escalating measures of intervention were to be undertaken.

Then the NCLB ceiling, so to speak, came crashing down on the principalship. I won't dwell on the wrong-headedness of NCLB. The truth is it could never work in a large, complex system. When it was replaced in 2015 with the Every Student Succeeds Act (ESSA), some breathing room was restored but still no hope for overall system change. Countries like Canada, Finland, South Korea, and Singapore fared better with less oppressive strategies, but I will maintain later in this chapter that progress on the main learning and well-being outcomes essential for the present and future could never be achieved under any number of variations of the present system—it is the system itself that must be transformed.

In the meantime (the last 100 years and more), no variations of the old system could possibly work: the autonomous principal, the micro-supervised deliverer, license to transform—nothing worked or could work on any scale. The consequences are disastrous: two-thirds of students bored or alienated; teachers alienated from their profession, and from the bureaucracy; parents disillusioned; technology rising without moral pedagogy; education playing no social role for the betterment of the planet or society; and principals run ragged. Time to turn to brand-new alternatives.

I consider *complexity thinking* (or, as I sometimes call it, simplexity) the most practical and powerful approach we have available. In the absence of complexity thinking, we have solutions that are either too simplistic (NCLB) or too complicated (artificial intelligence). We should never trust AI by itself—the solution is to partner with AI but be wary of putting it in the driver's seat.

Let's take two simplexity observations to pave the way to next steps. One is about *change process;* the other about *change content* (Figure 6.1). Once you get into complex territory with humans you can't order them to do something and expect good results. With respect to process, when conditions (solutions) get complex, complicatedness grinds things to a halt in the absence of human-led problem-solving.

So, what should be great content and great processes for *future making*? We don't have the space to write a detailed manifesto of the future (our principals' vignettes give us plenty of ideas for what this might entail). We do need to address the essence of the content and the process of what can only be called our desperately urgent future.

The content of the change is best stated as *the future of humanity*. What needs work, desperately so, is to improve the *human condition!* And while we are at it, we might as well

Figure 6.1 Change Process and Change Content

Change Process: ***Coercion never works!***

If its complex, supervision is not feasible; and coercion can never deliver on comprehension or deep skills–put another way, even if people were willing many probably wouldn't know how to do what was required or how to generate it.

Besides. there are better ways to convince people to consider something new (such as our 'use the group to change the group', channeled voluntarism, enabling the young to play a bigger part).

And furthermore, the resisters may be right (that the idea is not a good one; is flawed).

Change Content: ***Good ideas are everywhere***

You are more likely to find an array of good ideas, and good insights (what I call "nuance") in practices and its interstices closer to day-to-day work than you are within the group at the top. For the simplexity solutions required (the future is now), you need the commitment and ideas of those at the level of practice. We call it "joint determination," which, if done well, means people at all levels will be influential.

play it safe and power up the learning and well-being system to enable humans (individually, collaboratively, and collectively) to *flourish*.

There are signs that we are moving to a new system. We, and many others we know, have partnered with others in the field to develop a new system we call the *humanity paradigm*. It is based on four drivers: (1) well-being and learning; (2) combining social and artificial intelligence; (3) equality investments; and (4) systemness (Fullan & Quinn, forthcoming). Our deep learning model is busy (with practitioners around the world) spelling out and enacting the solution: new purpose and belonging, six global competencies (character, citizenship, collaboration, communication, creativity, and critical thinking), detailed pedagogies of engagement, new cultures at the school and middle levels, and, crucially, "new metrics" (including a partnership with the University of Melbourne's new metrics initiative) assessing the 6Cs, in effect replacing NCLB thinking once and for all. I am encouraged by the many lines of interest in making the humanity paradigm the centerpiece of the transformation. Indeed, the content of the change is becoming more clear and more evident with many more backers and implementers across the globe. The content includes greater equality for all, and greater empowerment for all (in the sense of influencing the system in ways that satisfy the vast majority of people) and their future aspirations. Alas, the forces of the status quo present a formidable bedrock of resistance. But I can't help but think that when a system blatantly does not work the forces of humanity and learned hopefulness may have a chance of breaking through to form durable new pathways.

As always, the most difficult and exciting part concerns the process because it involves changing the *culture of a system*—changing our old friend the 200-year-old 'grammar of schooling' (well, if you are a sociologist). I am going to illustrate the nature of these changes for four roles: principals, teachers, students, and parents and communities (remember—our best allies). Of course, this will have profound implications for all others at other levels upward because they will eventually like the change as well. More sophisticated power-driven strategies are also in our toolbox—more sophisticated because it entices and pushes more and more of those at the top to join in—even to lead—voluntarily or otherwise. We can start with the principal.

You might begin with our principal vignettes scattered throughout the book. Do these leaders strike you as stuck in the middle? Of course, they are not typical, but they show it can be done. With respect to the latter I believe that the time is right to dramatically improve the lot of principals as a

The Principal

What kind of job description is this?
Stuck in the middle
Losing control, yeah,
I'm all over the place

(Gerry Rafferty, Joe Egan)

single integrated strategy. If we go in this direction, we will discover that there is a huge amount of mutual empathy among the principals, teachers, students, parents, and communities who are working together. And better when there is a massive attraction to the changes that could be accomplished together. Again, review our principal vignettes. Do you think there is any doubt these principals and their teachers loved each other as they carried out enormously challenging work? Take the flip side: those situations—the majority actually—where principals and teachers hate their jobs and relationships with each other and would rather not put up with another day under the current conditions. How long do you think it would take the principals featured in this book to change the culture of other schools in terms of the creating radically different cultures?

In an overall sense, the strategy is to employ the three keys. More operationally, think of the solution along the following lines. Remember again who the best allies are: principals, teachers, students, parents, and communities. Rethink the relationship between teacher and principal, just like that of how teachers and students relate for best results, where authentic and meaningful change can be realized *regardless* for a moment what is happening at the state and federal level. In short, *bring the change in here instead of out there.* Principals and teachers in effective schools admit there is a power dynamic in school systems but refuse to let it define the relationship. Good teachers know there is a power relationship between themselves and students, but they rarely use it to get results (because power never gets lasting changes; there are better ways than coercion). Incumbent principals and teachers didn't ask for the power structure to be created. If they really want things to be different, acknowledge it exists, and demonstrate how you are going to be intentional in shifting it.

Most of the status quo comes from very fixed, external definitions of power, leadership, position. Move with your student and teacher partners to different definitions that are dynamic, internal, shared influence that guide, connect, and serve and generate new energy and great solutions. You don't need permission to do this. In cases of success, it is *the internal system* (school, community, region) that becomes the lead force proactively coping with and influencing *the external system* (policies, regulations). Principals are key to the rise of internal systems, which in turn could and should be a greater force for system transformation.

While you're at it, beware of solutions from above, that of the "I thought that was what you wanted" ilk. When teachers report that there should be more communication, they are not saying that they want more newsletters, more emails from administrators, and a district communications director. What teachers really mean is that they don't feel seen or heard; they want to be communicated with personally. Same for students. Western societies have a bad cultural habit of talking over/at/about kids without really listening to them. Another powerful role for the new principalship—liberate youth for the work of transforming learning and well-being in the new era.

When teachers worry about accountability, they may be referring to the district not being accountable as more people are becoming unhealthy on the job due to people becoming ill and related high turnover rates. In most hierarchical relationships, those at the top do most of the talking. Change that! Think of the lyric from the old rap song "check yo' self before you wreck yo' self." Are administrators doing most of the talking? Setting the parameters? Do you still try to conduct meetings like it was 2019? Are you actually getting buy-in or respect; or our people just being nice to you?

Notice that I have instigated the change from the bottom up—that is where most ideas are, where most of the required energy can and must be found. My point is that the most powerful momentum changers are found at the bottom and middle. The bonus is that as you start this upward energy flow, many of those at the middle and top will also start initiating such breakthrough strategies. The motto: there is nothing about the status quo that should be considered to be fixed. Start in here, not out there, and cause both to change. Such a strategy would foster much more joy and easy climate when people are good with each other. Focus on the goals, not the roles. When such a shift is made, people feel more like partners—not observers, or worse, victims in a bad game. Give up the false comfort of being in charge and enjoy the power of joint reform.

Finally, let me be clear about one matter. I am not saying that there are no examples of successful system-led reform at the district or country level. I am saying that they are few in number and in that case are exceptions. In this book, we are not seeking this and that ad hoc system change. It is widespread change in systemness that matters—how any system can best go about changing itself for the better in a short period of time and do so with lasting results and how most systems could end up doing this.

Before turning to the student, I thought we might take a short visit to Finland, the land where people are apparently nice to teachers. We won't find the solution there. Linda Darling-Hammond disabused us of this when she warned: "You can't fire your way to Finland!" Interestingly, while everyone lauds Finland's teachers, you find very little written about the principal in Finland. Two of our Finnish colleagues, Tapio Lahtero and Mikko Salonen (2022), just published (in English) a clear portrayal of *The Principal's Role at Finnish Schools: Leading Change for Foreseeable Cultures*. They found that education is valued at all levels, embraced by teachers, principals, and communities. The system is described in terms of five principles: the uniqueness of the student; the right to a good education; humanity, civilization, equity, and democracy; cultural diversity as an asset; and a sustainable way of life (Lahtero & Salonen, p. 9). Developing education requires a holistic approach. The role of the principal focuses on *school culture* defined in terms of *technical leadership*, *pedagogical leadership*, and *human leadership*. All members of the school community take part in building the school culture. When necessary, in situations of conflict, there is an external procedure with supportive external facilitators who act with the school to resolve problems.

Lahtero and Salonen conclude that "the central role of a principal is to initiate, sustain, and actively participate in the social processes of collaboration, goal setting and learning community building" (p. 16). Teams are at the heart of collaborative leadership. In 2019 a survey of teachers was conducted in Finland to assess the "impact of the new team model" in terms of whether it was working. Almost 98% of teachers felt that they could share their ideas with others; 95% felt heard (p. 49).

Finland has a way to go. The weaknesses were also revealing. Aspects identified were lack of community spirit at the school level; the need for more decision-making power and responsibility; not enough time for pedagogical discussions; and cooperation between teams need to be further developed (pp. 49–50). The authors seem to conclude, as I did earlier, that good "pedagogical leadership" by itself, at best, produces "the competent principal," not the transformative system leader (Chapter 3, p. 52). Nor does the "technical, pedagogical, human resources leadership" fit the full bill. We end up according to the authors with "a well-run school and a competent principal" (p. 59).

It turns out, according to Lahtero and Salonen, that the excellent principal is "competent plus": technical, pedagogical, human resources "plus" providing "symbolic" and "cultural leadership" (p. 63). Their overall conclusion is that "all members of the school community" should build the school culture (p. 74). Finally, the authors conclude that the whole set is a matter of layered cultures (leadership, school, local community, national) (Chapter 5, p. 78).

Why am I bothering you with Finland? I am with Linda Darling-Hammond. You can't borrow other people's culture. But this little sideshow makes a few helpful points. In the land where teachers are known to be uniformly good, it is because the country invested in it, and they cultivated leaders who enabled widespread quality. Second, principals were teacher facing, and that's probably a good thing (necessary but not sufficient).

Finally, they are possibly on the right track but have not yet gone far enough, which is to develop a more radical system transformation enabled by the three keys.

We are back then to the conclusion that just as we want teachers to enable students to experience engaging, dynamic, inclusive cultures humming with productivity, *enabled by teachers individually and collectively,* we require principals to interact similarly with teachers (parents and communities). Principals, if you haven't done it already, *turn inward like the principals in this book to be more effective outward!* Inward–outward is the force.

Recognize that principals must become experts in each of the three keys: spirit leaders; contextually literate; and systemness. Moreover, they must help *integrate* and *synthesize* the three. Developing each one feeds the other two so that together they create a single force.

Teachers

This is a book about the principal, so I am not going to go full bore on the other local roles of teachers, students, parents, and community members. However, key reciprocal points are crucial. Bottom-up change is an all-hands-on-deck proposition if we are going to transform the system. The obvious reciprocal change surrounding the teacher are teacher–teacher(s); teacher(s)–student; teacher(s)–parents and community; and teacher(s)–principal. These are pretty much parallel propositions.

If you are blessed with the kind of principals I featured in this book, go to town on the featured journey. Rewrite the hierarchical script. Partner with willing and compatible principals to change the culture. Together expand and deepen the agenda with students, parents, and community. Even if some principals seem reticent, help push them to the new relationships (the latter turn out to be more enjoyable and productive in most cases). Become more influential locally as you participate upward to change the system itself. Systemness change is the toughest problem you will ever have tackled. The only chance of success is upward generated, followed by consolidation at all levels.

If you are in a situation that is hopelessly wrong-headed about these matters, get your satisfaction from small pockets of success, or go elsewhere, or leave the profession. It's not your fault.

But don't give up too soon. Remember there are *Six Reasons to be Optimistic* and this is early "pandemic disruption" time. This is the right time to return to the agenda that Andy Hargreaves and I set out in detail in our 2012 book *Professional Capital*. We made the distinction between *business capital*, where big business and now big technology take over and run the show (in the *Drivers* paper I called this the *bloodless paradigm*; Fullan, 2021). Hargreaves and I contrasted the bloodless model with *professional capital*, where teachers with each other and their students do well in the present as they help create the future. Today we are still mired in the dominant role of big technology and business (see Broussard, forthcoming), but I also sense that the combination of new drivers (well-being, learning, combining social and artificial intelligence, quality investments, and new systems) could turn the tables. After all the best technologists in the world weren't born till 2000 (see Prensky, 2022)!

With respect to professional capital, some of the new change forces are potentially more favorable, but it will be a battle (of the decade, maybe the century). What I am writing in this book, and in this chapter, is an invitation to teachers to join in individually and collectively to develop the profession they never knew they wanted (but will recognize once the see it).

The Student

In this decade (2020s) is it possible we could witness, indeed foster on massive scale, a fundamental change in the role of the student in learning and well-being, and most critically in *the student as changemaker—en masse!* Everything I have said in this book points to and confirms this as a desirable pathway forward. Children from 3 years up (actually younger) will be the changemakers of the present for the future. Remember, the radical change theme and underpinning is about humanity and the human condition. Young people gravitate to this theme individually, in small groups, and in numbers. They want to partner with like-minded adults. They can't help but employ technology in this quest. And they worry about the human condition and its future—partly out of self-interest and partly because they know no limits. They instinctively feel that the universe can destroy us or enable itself and us to flourish. More and more of the youth would rather work on the latter. They like the question—what's life for anyway? The most powerful phrase we have ever coined, coming directly from our work in the last eight years, what we believe is the tacit potential of every child, with the right experience—the overt desire—*let me engage the world, change the world!* The three keys for maximizing impact are devoted to that future reality.

Parents and Community

The last local partner is parents and the community. This component has not been a big part of the history of educational reform (notice I said "big part"—there have been parent and community movements that have come and gone). Part of the pandemic windfall (or downfall, depending on how it turns out), parents and community are part of the "best allies" group. The new community schools (CS) movement in California should give new momentum. CS is about reducing poverty and hardship, as it builds community and competency-based learning. Again, this is part and parcel of the three keys and the new principalship.

Where to from Here

I have not tackled the overall system and how to transform it. A clear subtext of this book is that we fundamentally have the wrong paradigm or model. We have a bloodless system: it is more like que sera, sera (with apologies to Doris Day), whereas we need a deliberate, deep humanity paradigm (Fullan & Quinn, forthcoming). Our eight principals would fit very nicely in the new model. Indeed, they would be first in line to lead the development of such a new system. I hope this book will be of direct help to incumbent principals to serve as internal change agents realizing that they are paving the way to a different future beyond their individual schools.

Most people on the planet still wake up every day to face a terrible world. The slow boats ensconced for the past 200 years have been moving bit by bit to erode a passive globe when it comes to the big things: climate, racism, inequality, relationship with strangers, and overall inhumanity. I don't know whether our ancestors ever thought consciously about evolution (certainly indigenous communities did and do) in terms of where the universe and the planet might be going—and what they could do about it. I am pretty sure that rapidly increasing numbers of current 3–18-year-olds worry about the present and think the future is approaching with frightening alacrity. The percentage of youth who want to do something about the present and future for the betterment of themselves and all must be at an all-time high.

We need a new approach to system change. So far, system change has been a combination of top-down forces from dictators or elected leaders or from evolution (i.e., whatever happens, happens). From 2003 to 2013, I was part of system change in Ontario, where I worked as education advisor for Premier Dalton McGuinty, which has a population of some 13 million people, 2 million students, and 5,000 schools. We initiated literacy numeracy, high school reform from the top. This reform was considered a success given the goals and the parameters of the day, but I now know that top-down change (even with a spirit of partnership) would not work in 2023 for two big reasons: in most jurisdictions there is little continuity of leadership at the top; and, more significantly, the problems have become so complex and deeply dynamic that they simply cannot be solved from the top.

Many people at all levels—the very young for one example—have come to the conclusion that leadership at and from the top does and cannot work. At times of paradigm shift (where the old model no longer works, and cannot be fixed), and the new model has yet been well developed there comes ever stronger interest in new models. At the beginning of such disruption there are typically several new models being pursued all of which are at an early *inchoate* stage. I believe that this is where we are now. Things are failing, people are panicking, and most everyone is anxious. A new model of change is implicit in my treatment of the new principalship 2.0.

I apologize for being excessively cryptic here, but at this stage I expect the reader to begin the deep thinking. I can only hint at the direction that we have been going in with more and more clarity, additionally stimulated by the pandemic, and by those working for similar new directions. The starting point is how to think about system change. Here is a big hint about how to go about it: *build the base* (e.g., the young, local groups); *mobilize the middle* (e.g., the neighborhood, regional agencies); *intrigue the top* (e.g., tempting system leaders to find out where promising things are happening). My guess is that the best principals would be good at this.

It is the case that educators, health care professionals, and indeed most of us are at near exhaustion with the relentless bombardment and cascade of physical, mental, and social ills that have pounded us over the past three years. Never in our lifetimes has so much grief descended on us individually and collectively. If there is ever to be a turning point it needs to be now—2023. We have many more resources than we realize to fight back and fight forward. It could be the medicine that we need as humans, what I call, learned hopefulness. Could there ever be a better time to be alive and aware of the dangers while *having a chance to do something about it*? I think not. Let the young rise to help lead the way from day one. Spirit work, contextual literacy, systemness: use the three keys to open a new universe!

REFERENCES

Broussard, M. (in press). *More Than a Glitch: Confronting Race, Gender, and Ability Bias in Tech*. Cambridge, MA: MIT Press.

Brighouse, T., and M. Waters (2021). *About Our Schools: Improving on Previous Best*. Wales, UK: Crown Publishing Company.

British Columbia School Superintendents Association (2022). *Leadership Competencies*. Vancouver B.C: Author.

Campero, A. (2019). *Genes vs Culture vs Consciousness*. Lexington, KY: Author.

Cantor, P., and D. Osher (2021). *The Science of Learning and Development*. London: Routledge.

DuFour, R., and R. Marzano (2009). High Leverage Strategies for Principal Leadership. *Educational Leadership* 66(5): 62–68.

Dufour, R., and M. Mattos (2013). How Do Principals Really Improve Schools? *Educational Leadership* 70(7): 34–40.

Fullan, M. (2014). *The Principal: Three Keys for Maximizing Impact*. San Francisco, CA: Jossey-Bass.

Fullan, M. (2019). *Nuance: Why Some Leaders Succeed and Others Fail.* Thousand Oaks, CA: Corwin.

Fullan, M. (2021). *The Right Drivers for Whole System Success.* Seminar Series. Melbourne, AU: Center for Strategic Education.

Fullan, M. (2022a). *Six Reasons to be Optimistic About Learning in 2022.* Bethesda, MD: Education Week; Toronto, Ontario: New Pedagogies for Deep Learning.

Fullan, M. (2022b). *Here Are 6 Reasons Our Students Should Be Seen as Changemakers.* Bethesda, MD, Education Week, September 6.

Fullan, M., and M. Edwards (2022). *Spirit Work and the Science of Collaboration.* Thousand Oaks, CA: Corwin.

Fullan, M., and M. Pinchot (2018, March). The Fast Track to Sustainable Turnaround. *Educational Leadership*, pp. 48–54.

Fullan, M., J. Quinn, and J. McEachen (2018). *Deep Learning: Engage the World Change the World.* Thousand Oaks, CA: Corwin.

Fullan, M., and M. J. Gallagher (2020). *The Devil Is in the Details: System Solutions for Equity, Excellence, & Student Well-Being.* Thousand Oaks, CA: Corwin.

Fullan, M., B. Spillane, and B. Fullan (2022). Commentary: Connected Autonomy. *Journal of Professional Capital and Community* 7(4):329–333.

Fullan, M., D. Osher, K. Junk, and J. Malloy (2022). *Supporting Student Well-Being and Learning in Challenging*

Times: A Transition Tool. Arlington, VA: American Institute for Research.

Fullan, M., and J. Quinn (forthcoming). *The Drivers: Transforming the Future of Well-Being and Learning*. Thousand Oaks, CA: Corwin.

Hargreaves, A., and M. Fullan (2012). *Professional Capital: Transforming Teaching in Every School*. New York, NY: Teachers College Press.

Hannon, V., and J. Temperley (2022). *Futureschool*. London: Routledge.

Ikler, J. (2021a). Unleashing the Power of a Team of Teacher Leaders (Michelle Pinchot). https://www.queticocoaching.com/blog/2021/6/9/getting-unstuck-182-unleashing-the-power-of-a-team-of-teacher-leaders

Ikler, J. (2021b). Tending the Garden of Future Leaders (Janani Pathy). https://www.queticocoaching.com/blog/2021/6/9/getting-unstuck-192-tending-the-garden-of-future-leaders

Isaacson, W. (2017). *Leonardo da Vinci*. New York: Simon & Schuster.

Kaplan, R., and R. Kaiser (2013). *Fear Your Strengths*. San Francisco, CA: Berrett-Koehler.

Kirp, D. (2013). *Improbable Scholars*. New York: Oxford University Press.

Kirp, D. (2022). *Disrupting Disruption*. New York: Oxford University Press.

Kirtman, L. (2013). *Leadership and Teams*. Upper Saddle River, NJ: Pearson Education.

Kirtman, L. (2021). *Research Findings on Leadership Effectiveness That Might Surprise You*. Unpublished manuscript.

Lahtero, T., and M. Salonen (2022). *The Principal's Role at Finnish Schools*. Helsinki: Professional Publishing Finland Oy.

Malin, H. (2018). *Teaching for Purpose*. Cambridge, MA: Harvard University Press.

Martin, R., and S. Osberg (2015). *Getting Beyond Better*. Boston, MA: Harvard Business School Press.

National Commission on Excellence in Education (1983). *A Nation at Risk*. Washington, DC: Author.

New Jersey Department of Education (2013). *Student growth objectives: Developing and using practical measures of student learning*. Trenton, NJ. Author.

New Pedagogies for Deep Learning (NPDL) (2022). *Defying Pandemic Gravity*. Toronto, Ontario.

Prensky, M. (2022). *Empowered!: Re-framing "Growing Up" for a New Age*. Marc Prensky and the Global Ministry of Empowerment, Accomplishment, and Impact. Palo Alto, CA.

Putnam, R., and S. Garrett (2020). *Upswing*. New York: Simon & Schuster.

Quinn, J., J. McEachen, M. Fullan, M. Gardner, and M. Drummy (2020). *Dive into Deep Learning: Tools for Engagement*. Thousand Oaks, CA: Corwin.

Robinson, V., C. Lloyd, and K. Rowe (2008). The Impact of Leadership on Student Outcomes. *Education Administration Quarterly* 44: 635–674.

Senge, P. (1990). *The Fifth Discipline*. New York: Doubleday.

Sullivan, E. T. (2022). *Principals on the Brink of Breakdown*. EdSurge Newsletter. American Principal Survey. Available at http://www.edsurge.com

Vista Unified School District (2022). *Community Schools* Vista Unified School District.

ACKNOWLEDGMENTS

I CAN'T DO JUSTICE TO THE HELP, SUPPORT, AND THINKING that I have received in developing this book. On every front I have been blessed by people who were willing to give me their best ideas and insights under conditions of massive pressure and overload. Never has there been such a bombardment of challenges, crises, desperation, heroic actions, potential breakthrough ideas, confusion, and excitement as we are witnessing in the 2018 to 2023 period.

I thank the thousands of principals we know and work with from at least 20 countries, and those who work with them locally. I thank the teachers, students, and parents who, with their principals and senior administrators, are each other's best allies at this crucial time in our evolution. Thank you to Claudia Cuttress, who shepherded yet another book through the speedy complexities of production while producing scores of quality materials as we test, produce, and disseminate the ideas. Nobody combines speed, quality, and creativity better than Claudia.

On the broader front, I have amazing team members: the core deep learning and system teams listed here alphabetically: Jean Clinton, Max Drummy, Mary Jean Gallagher, Mag Gardner,

Bill Hogarth, Joanne Quinn, Santiago Rincón-Gallardo, Joanna Rizzotto, and two of my sons, Josh and Bailey Fullan. Beyond the team, there are too many great colleagues to mention—people all over the globe doing spirit work with aplomb and unselfish collaboration. Thanks to Mark Edwards for *Spirit Work* and to Brendan Spillane for *Contextual Literacy* and *Connected Autonomy*. Thank you to my wife, Wendy Marshall, who supports and helps develop several generations of us—call her principal in residence.

It's great to be back with the Jossey-Bass crew. Ashante Thomas and her editorial team not only have made *Principal 2.0* better all through production but also have been comprehensively proactive with innovative ideas to develop, position, market, and otherwise feature this book. Finally, a deep thank you to the Stuart Foundation for supporting our system work over the years.

I am fortunate in so many ways. Thank you all.

ABOUT THE AUTHOR

Michael Fullan, Ph.D., Order of Canada, is Professor Emeritus and former dean, OISE/University of Toronto and co-director of New Pedagogies for Deep Learning (NPDL).

A world authority on educational change and system transformation, Fullan works at all levels of the system from students to policymakers. He is an award-winning author whose books have been published in several languages. He holds honorary doctorates from five universities around the world.

INDEX